Where Menhaden Was King

The Lewes Fishing Industry 1883-1966

Where Menhaden Was King

The Lewes Fishing Industry
1883-1966

Thomas Elton Brown, Ph.D.

Lewes Historical Society

©2022 Lewes Historical Society
All Rights reserved

Published by Lewes Historical Society
110 Shipcarpenter Street
Lewes, Delaware 19958

www.historiclewes.org

April 2022

ISBN 978-0-578-39982-9

Manufactured in the United States

Cover Design and Layout by Kevin McLaughlin/KMDesign, Inc.
Front Cover: Gouache Painting of Menhaden by Joanne K. Guilfoil
Back Cover: *Steamin into Lewes* by Steve Rogers, Gift of Carl Wisler & Midge Smith, Digital Photograph by Peninsula Gallery

DEDICATED TO
JAMES H. LEMLY JR.
1948 – 2008

HE TOUCHED MANY HEARTS
HE CAPTURED MINE

Contents

Preface viii
Introduction 1
Chapter 1: The Fish No One Knows 5
Chapter 2: Catching and Processing Menhaden 8
Chapter 3: Black and White Work Side-by-Side 14
Chapter 4: The Menhaden Industry in Lewes Begins 21
Chapter 5: A Tale of Two Home Companies 30
Chapter 6: The Lewes Fisheries Company 34
Chapter 7: More Legal Troubles for Lofland 40
Chapter 8: It's in the Lease 46
Chapter 9: There Will Be Plenty of Fish 52
Chapter 10: Something Fishy in Politics 59
Chapter 11: The People Speak 67
Chapter 12: The Fight Continues 73
Chapter 13: A Critical Industry Survives 106
Chapter 14: Organizing the Smith Companies 113
Chapter 15: Research and Development 120
Chapter 16: The Future Looked Promising 124
Chapter 17: The Historic Charm of Lewes Emerges 134
Appendix A 141
Endnotes 148
Index 169

Preface

I am an historian by training and trade, having spent over thirty years working at the National Archives in Washington, D.C. I retired fifteen years ago and moved to the Delaware beaches. I no longer wanted to be employed, but I was not ready to stop working. So as not to waste my time, I touched base with my colleagues throughout the United States who were knowledgeable about archives and historical activities on the Eastern Shore. I asked them where I should volunteer. Everyone, without fail, told me that it should be the Lewes Historical Society because, they explained, it has a stellar reputation as a professionally managed organization responsible for preserving a heritage of a community worthy of preservation.

I made an appointment with Mike DiPaolo, then the executive director of the Society. In discussing my background and interests, I tried to hide my superficial knowledge of the history of Lewes. Since we were at the end of the summer season, being a volunteer docent at one of the Society's buildings or leading one of the Society's tours was not possible. In absence of such activities, he asked if I would do some research until a more formal volunteer activity became available the next summer. Hearing me agree, Mike suggested that I try to figure out what were the menhaden companies in Lewes and how they were related to each other. Mike said that he kept seeing the names of various companies, particularly before 1920, and could not figure out when they started and ended or if they ever even had a factory in Lewes. Such confusion is understandable when one realizes that the Lewes Fisheries Company morphed into the Lewes Fish Oil and Fertilizer Company and then into the Lewes Fertilizer Company. Also, Lewes hosted a Seacoast Products Company and a Seacoast Products Incorporated, two totally different businesses. Or the Delaware Fish Oil and Fertilizer Company was a separate entity from the Delaware Fish Oil Company, which was mistakenly called Delaware Fisheries Company. Mike readily admitted that he did not know of any sources on the early companies but suggested that I start off with the Society's Journal and its articles on the fishing industry and see where that would take me. Without hesitation, I agreed to see what I could find out.

In all honesty, I immediately went home and did a Google search for "menhaden." I had never heard of it before that morning but thought that it was a fish of some kind judging from the clues in my conversation with Mike. I spent that off-season in the Society's library trying to find out about early commercial fishing in Lewes. The next summer, I did become a docent with a traditional assignment of explaining to visitors the U.S. Life Saving Service at the boat house along the Lewes-Rehoboth canal and later leading Maritime History Walking Tours of Lewes. In the off-season, I continued my research into the perplexing history of the early menhaden companies. My research expanded to the history of all the companies and people of the Lewes menhaden industry from the first plant in 1883 to the closure of the last in 1966.

Microfilmed newspapers became my pastime, whether they were the *Delaware Coast News* at the Rehoboth Public Library, the *Wilmington News Journal* at Delaware Public Archives, or the *Milford Chronicle* at the Milford Public Library. Since the Town of Lewes controlled the bayfront from the canal to Cape Henlopen, its town commissioners leased the land for the factories. The minutes of the Lewes commissioners from 1883 to 1966 were available at the Lewes city hall. For some reason that I have never really understood, the leases the town awarded to the owners of the fish plants were interfiled with real property transfers at the Recorder of Deeds in the basement of the Sussex County Courthouse in Georgetown. When Chancery Court cases entered the narrative or the state of Delaware became involved, I found myself in the research room of the Delaware Public Archives. Twice the Army Corps of Engineers became involved and held hearings, and my experience at the National Archives helped me to pinpoint where the transcripts of those hearings could be located.

A decade has passed since I first learned what a "menhaden" is. Lest one assume that I spent ten years focused only on the Lewes menhaden factories, other activities occupied great chunks of my time. Fortunately, this was a hobby, an avocation. As I would often explain, I rekindled my graduate school love affair with old paper.

Another project also interfered with my menhaden research when Hazell Melson Smith, Otis Smith's widow, donated prior to her passing some of her late husband's materials to the Society. With my archival experience and interest in the Lewes menhaden history, Mike DiPaolo asked me to arrange and catalog the 30 boxes of materials into an archival inventory. I leapt at the opportunity. Without a doubt, my work with Smith's papers and records did inform my research into the later years of the Lewes fish plants. More importantly, the task gave me an insight into and an appreciation of Otis Smith's myriad involvements far beyond his fish factories. An example of this legacy is found in my article, "Otis Smith: An Unlikely Civil Rights Pioneer," in Lewes History: Journal of the Lewes Historical Society (2019) which discusses the significance of his drive in 1962 to Selbyville to attempt to integrate a local eatery. This trip was the first proactive, official step that the state of Delaware ever took to end racial segregation. So, the reader may be disappointed with my history of the menhaden business in Lewes because it includes little about Otis Smith beyond the menhaden business. My aim was so focused on his operation of the fish factories that I only mention in passing that he was the Lewes mayor from 1950 to 1968. Rather, Smith is worthy of a separate study that focuses solely on him.

A similar disappointment may be the limited history of the African American community in Lewes. Again, I feel it needs a separate study. The fish factories brought into Lewes a significant number of black migrant workers from the 1920s to the 1960s. Most of them returned to their homes in North Carolina and Virginia after the season ended, but some did stay and became Lewestowners. Their legacy as both seasonal and full-time residents remains to be written. How the temporary influx during the fishing season impacted the Black community, other than the noted jazz venue, Black Cat Club, needs exploration. Totally unanswered is the diaspora of African American residents from Lewes following the demise of the menhaden plants.

I am indebted to many people for the help they gave me. Mike DiPaolo, who suggested that I research the early companies. In the ensuing years, he directed me to many sources in the Lewes Historical Society collections in response to my specific questions, read through the full manuscript and offered knowledgeable insights, and conceptualized the chart of the fish companies by year. Two others who read the early drafts and provided insightful comments and suggestions for additional sources were Hazel Brittingham, a Lewes native who has a thorough knowledge of Lewes history, and Robert Kennedy Jr., who worked for Fish Products Company and has made the history of the Lewes menhaden fishery an avocation. At the Lewes Historical Society, its editor, Bill Meehan, was instrumental in rearranging the chapters of the first draft, focusing each of them on a topic, and providing an overall structure and purpose. He also compensated for my life-long inattention to grammatical details and for my habitual inclusion of unnecessary details. Denise Clemons, Society's archivist and trustee, supplied significant research assistance as she located obscure facts to answer my questions. Jim Abbott, the Society's Executive Director, arranged for the organization's full support. The chair of the Society's Board of Trustees, Elizabeth Owen, has fully endorsed Jim's effort to promote the scholarly exploration of Lewes history, including this work. The entire staff at the Delaware Public Archives could not have been more professional and helpful. There, Margaret Raubacher Dunhamas steered me through the labyrinth of textual records and frequently called my attention to relevant materials. I would like to acknowledge the staffs of the National Archives at Philadelphia, the Lewes Public Library, the Rehoboth Public Library, and the Milford Public Library.

I am also thankful to many friends and even strangers who endured the boredom of my fish stories for the past decade. I cannot conclude this list without acknowledging Bill Coughlin. He has stood by my side since October 2018 and has encouraged me in deed and in word to bring this history to a successful conclusion.

Despite all the assistance I received, I alone am responsible for the deficiencies in this study.

TEB
Palm Springs, CA
January 1, 2022

The Lewes Historical Society acknowledges Office Administrator Carolann Wolansky; manuscript readers David F. Riddick, Jane Harrison, and Barbara Garrity-Blake; amanuensis Denise Perez; interns Tad Glasscock, Brayden Moore, and Holly Wright; designer Kevin McLaughlin; and indexer Liz Coelho. We especially are grateful for Bill Meehan's professional management of this project from start to finish.

LHS
Lewes, DE
January 1, 2022

Introduction

"Rehoboth by the sea. Lewes by the smell." This quip from the 1950s extolled Rehoboth Beach as a resort and belittled Lewes for its permeating odor of dead fish. As with most humor, it contains more than a grain of truth. From June to October during the 1950s, Lewes had two fish factories that processed daily around two million pounds of a bony, oily fish called Atlantic menhaden. Workers cooked the raw menhaden to extract the fish oil, dried the carcasses, and ground the remains into pulverized bones and flesh, called fish meal, in a process now called "reduction." The overpowering stench from the fish factories pervades the history of Lewes during the first half of the twentieth century. This odor contrasted sharply with what Delaware historian Carol Hoffecker described as "the sweet aroma of the trees" that had greeted the Dutch explorers four centuries earlier. The stench also conflicts with the charming Lewes of today, whose wonderful historic district and architecture dating back to the 1600s juxtaposes Delaware's most popular state park that attracts over one million visitors each year.[1]

Justifying the rancid air of Lewes was the multitude of practical uses for the fish oil and the fish meal processed there. Rachael Carson, a marine biologist and noted conservationist, summarized the myriad uses: "Almost every person in the United States has at some time eaten, used or worn something made from menhaden." Native Americans were the first to use menhaden, mainly as fertilizer. At Plymouth, colonists learned from the Native Americans this original use of menhaden. Later, in addition to fertilizer, New England housewives in the early nineteenth century learned to boil menhaden in a vat until the oil rose to the surface for use in lamps. A menhaden factory in Rhode Island adopted the technique of boiling the fish and skimming the oil off the water's surface but disposing of the rest. Soon, menhaden oil plants dotted the coast from Maine to New York. Both the housewives and the first factories relied on shore-based nets or seines to haul in the fish. After the development in 1845 of the purse seine, a net to haul in schools from the ship, the fishermen could bring in larger catches farther from the shore.[2]

As whale oil became increasingly scarce and expensive, commercial processing of menhaden into oil as a substitute spiraled upward. It quickly replaced whale oil not only as an illuminant but also as a lubricant and industrial additive, and the industry began to reduce the number of carcasses drained of their oil into fish meal. Immediately after the Civil War, the industry established factories in the Chesapeake Bay and in the North Carolina coastal areas. Following World War I, with the development of the fish reduction process and chemists creating novel concoctions for fertilizers, the use of menhaden meal as an ingredient in animal feed primarily for poultry and swine began to overtake its use as a fertilizer. Since the end of the Lewes menhaden industry in 1966, fish meal and oil also have found their way into pet foods and aquaculture.[3]

New uses were constantly developed for menhaden oil. As a lubricant or industrial additive, it could replace or adulterate more expensive but readily available mineral oils, vegetable oils, coal oils, lard, kerosene and, very briefly, petroleum. As a drying oil, it is used in oil-based paints, varnishes, linoleum, caulking compounds, putties, soaps, and inks. This versatile oil finds its way into waterproofing fabrics and is also used in European oleo margarines and in U.S. pharmaceuticals. As a glycerin needed for munitions, menhaden processing was designated a "critical industry" in World War II. Cosmetics and soaps also consume sizeable quantities. A less delicate output comes from its use in tempering steel and tanning leather. In the 1970s, menhaden began to be used as bait for other fish by sport fishermen and commercial fishermen, especially in the blue crab fishery in the Chesapeake Bay and the lobster fishery in the northern Atlantic.[4]

About twenty years ago, the Federal Food and Drug Administration (FDA) approved menhaden oil for human consumption because it is rich in omega-3 fatty acids, which have a variety of health benefits. As these uses became better known, the demand for menhaden oil continued to increase. Today, a growing number of dietary supplements promote omega-3 as an ingredient and most of it comes from the fatty acids in menhaden oil. Following this lead, manufacturers have incorporated omega-3 fatty acids into beverages and foods.[5]

Another recurrent theme in the history of the Lewes menhaden industry, besides the smell, is the fish factories' relationship with the Lewes government, which made them part of the political fabric of the town. From colonial times, the land from the Lewes-Rehoboth Canal to the Atlantic Ocean was considered property of the town and, beginning in the late nineteenth century, state law required anyone occupying beach land east of the canal along what is Delaware Bay to obtain a lease. For a prospective entrepreneur to start a fish factory, the initial step therefore was to negotiate a lease with the town, effectively creating a tenant-landlord relationship. In all other areas on the Atlantic and Gulf coasts, menhaden fishery entrepreneurs purchased a plot of land and built a factory subject only to the generally lax zoning regulations. In Lewes, however, each factory needed explicit approval from the town by obtaining a lease agreement from the commissioners.

This tenant-landlord connection led the fish plants into involvement with the town's politics. Before the turn of the century, politicians who lost an election began accusing non-resident plant owners of contributing to their opponents' campaigns and telling employees for whom to vote. This carried over into the twentieth century, when two mayors were concurrently presidents of fish factories, one for over a decade and the another for nearly two decades. At times, members of the boards of directors served on the town commission. In at least two hotly contested elections, the future of the menhaden enterprise in Lewes was the decisive issue.[6]

The reliance on African American labor is a third element in the Lewes menhaden enterprise. Menhaden operations were physically intensive and depended heavily on back-breaking labor whether aboard a fishing vessel or in an on-shore factory. "In many ways, the menhaden industry is continuing the tradition of African American maritime fishing extending back before the Civil War," historian David Celeski commented. "More than any other industry, the menhaden industry carried that tradition of African American fishing in American life into the modern era." While he was primarily referring to the menhaden industry in Virginia and North Carolina, the tradition moved north to its Lewes counterpart after World War I. Prior to the war, the Lewes factories and ships recruited Portuguese, German, Irish, Polish, and Norwegian immigrants brought mainly from Baltimore and Philadelphia. With a decline in immigration and greater reliance on fishing vessels from Virginia, African Americans assumed a greater role in the Lewes labor force. While the officers on the ships and the supervisors in the factories were primarily White, the laborers on both sea and land were

Black. These racial walls were frequently breached when some Whites labored side-by-side with their Black crew mates and factory hands.[7]

With the support of town officials and the sweat of African American seamen and factory workers, the Lewes menhaden enterprise thrived until it reached its height in the 1950s. Then with landings of more than 200 million pounds of fish annually, Lewes laid its claim as the number one fishing port in the country. When the fish businesses hired locals to provision the ships and mess halls and to furnish skilled labor for the repair and maintenance of the physical factory complex, the impact rippled through the Lewes economy. Today, a sign in a park in Lewes summarizes it: "Where menhaden was king."

Chapter 1

The Fish No One Knows

The most critical element of the Lewes menhaden industry was obviously the menhaden itself. An Atlantic menhaden (*Brevoortia tyrannus*), when fully mature, is an eight-to-twelve-inch fish and weighs three-quarters of a pound to one pound. Silvery in color with a distinct black shoulder spot behind its gill opening, it is a member of the herring family. The fish possesses an unappetizing texture and smell primarily because of the slimy, putrid oil that covers its scales. Because it has little meat packed on its tiny bones, a menhaden would never find itself on a menu as a "food fish." This absence from restaurant menus has made it one of the least known fish. The lack of public recognition may be the reason for the number of nicknames for menhaden; it may have more monikers than any other species. In Virginia, menhaden are "bughead," "bugfish," "oldwife," "alewife," "greentail," and "chebog." Delaware adds "mossbunker" to the list. Connecticut shortened this to just "bunker" and offers up the nicknames of "whitefish," "bonyfish," and "hardhead." North Carolinians use "fatback" and "pogy." Some refer to the species as "spot" or "spot fish" because of the dark spot behind the gills, and others use "bug-fish" or "bug-head" because of a parasitic crustacean frequently found in its mouth. The name "menhaden" itself derives from *munnawhatteaug*, a Native American term for "that which enriches the earth."[8]

The life cycle of the menhaden begins with spawning, primarily along the Continental Shelf in shallow and flat waters from 260 feet to 460 feet deep and lying one or two miles off the Atlantic Coast from Miami to Cape Cod but also in the Chesapeake Bay. The timing for menhaden spawning varies by geography; it occurs throughout most of the year south of Delaware Bay but only in the warmer months north of the Bay. Female menhaden produce their eggs several times a year and can produce 40,000 to 700,000 eggs depending on her age. The eggs float to the surface, where they are fertilized and hatch within two days. The winds and tidal waves carry the larvae into the estuaries from Cape Cod to Cape Canaveral, such as the Delaware Bay and the Chesapeake Bay. The larvae are pushed into the tributaries flowing into the bays, inlets, and sounds to near the upper limit of the salt water.[9]

The tidal journey is perilous for the larvae. Drifting jelly fish and comb jellies can consume millions of the embryonic menhaden. The cavernous mouths of other planktivores, such as some species of sharks and whales, are lethal to large swaths of the floating larvae. Schools of any of the herring family are deadly to whole broods. If not eaten, larvae may not make it to their estuarine nursery due to vagaries of ocean waters, turbulence from storms, and unpredictable currents. A two- or three-day cold snap can abruptly stop their journey. Only an infinitesimal remnant of the eggs originally spawned arrive at the estuarine nursery, where the slender transparent organisms mature into juveniles that resemble adult menhaden and then to mature menhaden. In the autumn, they congregate in the estuary, and most move into the ocean where they will join a pre-existing school.[10]

Atlantic menhaden have no teeth; they are filter feeders, meaning that they collect food by filtering water through gill arches and gill rakers. Atlantic menhaden's diet is plankton, a variety of small organisms in water that cannot propel themselves. The type of plankton eaten depends on the size of their gill rakers, which change as menhaden age. Fish under the age of one have smaller rakers and feed primarily on microscopic plankton called phytoplankton. As they age and their gill rakers grow larger, menhaden shift their diet to larger plankton called zooplankton. Plankton live near the surface, and there one finds the menhaden. The menhaden need more oxygen than many other species, which also entices the menhaden to swim close to the ocean's surface. Because menhaden desire water between 60° F and 70° F, they migrate in the shallow depths off the Atlantic coast, from south to north in the spring, then reverse directions in the fall. After a winter dispersed off the Florida coast, menhaden reassemble in late March and early June into schools for the trip north. The older menhaden travel the farthest, reaching Narragansett Bay by May and the Gulf of Maine by June, which distributes the population from Maine to Florida. In September, the reverse migration begins, and the schools reach Virginia and North Carolina by November and December. This pattern gives rise to two fishing seasons. Between April and September, the "summer fishery" extends from North Carolina north. During the last three months of the year, the "fall fishery" is limited from North Carolina to Northern Florida. When migrating, the fish swim tightly packed side-by-side in immense schools, numbering in the hundreds of thousands, spreading across the ocean surface in expanses the size of football fields and descending up to 100 feet deep.[11]

Menhaden actually play an important ecological role in the ocean, providing a vital link between lower and upper levels of the food web. As consumers of planktonic organisms such as algae and zooplankton, menhaden help integrate critical microorganisms into the ocean's web. Atlantic menhaden are "forage fish" or food for larger species. Adult menhaden are prey for at least seventy-nine species of bigger fish (e.g., striper bass, mackerel, weakfish, bluefish, pollock, cod, silver hake, tuna, swordfish, and a variety of sharks), marine mammals (e.g., dolphins, humpback whales), birds (e.g., loons, osprey, eagles, gulls), and even reptiles (e.g., loggerhead turtles). In one of the early scientific studies of the species, G. Brown Goode, a Smithsonian ichthyologist, commented in 1880: "Their mission is unmistakably to be eaten."[12]

That said, it may be the menhaden's role in cleaning the ocean may be even more important.* As thousands of tightly packed menhaden slowly move across the surface of oceans, each fish has its mouth open, filtering four to six gallons of sea water each minute. Trapped in the gill rakers are the plankton as well as microscopic pollutants. Garbage in the waters of the continental shelf either floats to the surface or sinks to the bottom. If floating to the surface, the menhaden will remove it as the oysters do for the impurities that sink to the bottom. H. Bruce Franklin summarized this ecosystem: "They are filter feeders that live primarily on tiny even microscopic plants and other suspended matter, much of it indigestible or toxic to most other aquatic animals. Dense schools of menhaden, sometimes numbering in the hundreds of thousands, pour through these waters, toothless mouths agape, slurping up plankton, cellulose, and just plain detritus like a colossal submarine vacuum cleaner as wide as a city block and as deep as a train tunnel." Franklin characterized the menhaden as the "liver of the sea," and his representation of the species as "the most important fish in the sea" is not much of an overstatement.[13]

---

*Harrison points out, "The extent to which menhaden, a filter-feeding species, contributes to water quality is subject to scientific debate. Recent research conducted by the Virginia Institute of Marine Sciences suggests that filter feeding by menhaden has little net effect on overall water quality in the Chesapeake Bay." Harrison, "Menhaden: Big Questions About Little Fish," n.p.

Chapter 2

Catching and Processing Menhaden

Before a glow appeared in the eastern sky, menhaden vessels would set out from the factory's pier in search of their catch. As they negotiated the open sea, captains and first mates scaled the rope ladders to the top of the tall crow's nest, the distinctive feature of a menhaden vessel. From that perspective, the officers could scan a wide area of the ocean's surface.

Menhaden ships have run from 50 feet long in the nineteenth century up to 150 feet long in the twentieth century. Beginning with wind-and-sail schooners before the Civil War, the menhaden enterprise had moved by the end of the century to larger wind-powered sloops to coal-powered steamers to the diesel driven craft of the twentieth century. In time, the wooden vessels were replaced with steel. The original sloops had a crew of about ten, maxing out at around forty-two men aboard the wooden steamers in the 1930s but dropping to twenty-eight due to technological advances. The changing technologies meant that at menhaden piers along the Atlantic coast one could find more than one type of ship. Common attributes of all menhaden vessels were their wide hulls and shallow drafts. Wide hulls allowed the storage of large menhaden catches, space for 180,000 fish in the nineteenth century to more than a million fish during the height of the industry. The shallow drafts permitted ships, bulging with fish, to dock next to piers to unload their catches.[14]

From the vantage of the looming crow's nest, the captain and first mate would eye the ocean for a telltale sign of a menhaden school — an irregular reddish brown or purple mass looking like an oil spill the size of a football field moving slowly amid the blues and greens of the sea. The captain would shout "Fish!" or "Get Ready Below!" to launch the attack on the school in the distance. The captain and his mate raced down the crow's nest and joined much of the crew, who were divided into two 30-foot or 40-foot purse boats stored on davits aft; the captain in charge of one boat, the mate the other.

The "purse" refers to the purse seine, a mesh net about 1,200 feet long and 80 feet deep in the water. Within seven minutes after the sighting, the two purse boats moved carefully, side-by-side each with half of the net. A small skiff, called a "striker" boat, might have been ahead of them maneuvering to the far side of the school. The striker would beat or "strike" the water to keep menhaden from fleeing the oncoming purse boats. When the purse boats reached the menhaden, they separated with one sailing around the school in a clockwise direction and the other in a counterclockwise direction. As each moved away from the other purse boat, the purse seine was reeled out behind them. The seine had cork floats on the surface. The purse boats converged and completely encircled the school. When the boats met, the ends of the net were connected. A purse line through the lead sinkers at the bottom were connected to a 350-pound mass of lead called a "tom" weight. The tom was tossed into the ocean and would tighten the bottom of the net so the menhaden could not escape by diving under the net. The netted and trapped menhaden were called a "bunt." When attacked, the menhaden's main defense is to pack its schools as tightly as possible, unwittingly helping the crew to tighten the bunt even more.[15]

The captain then ordered the pilot of the mother ship to maneuver beside the two purse boats to make a triangle out of the three boats. Before a mechanizing process in the late 1950s, the crew worked manually and began the hard work of pulling the purse netting back into the boats ever tightening the bunt. Initially pulling the net into a bunt of fish was easy with only fathoms of empty net to pull up. As the bunt slightly constricted to allow the mother ship to form the iconic triangle of menhaden boats, the hard work of raising the net filled with hundreds of thousands of menhaden began. The crew worked hand-over-hand, achieving its by laboring in unison. To maintain this coordination, the bunt pullers, primarily African Americans, sang their unique, sometimes bawdy, chanteys and worked in rhythm to the tempo.

These chanteys are an enduring and endearing legacy of the menhaden enterprise. The chantey tradition started in the Northern Neck of Virginia and along the North Carolina coast when the first menhaden plants there began using African American laborers. These songs inherited the antebellum South tradition of slaves singing while toiling in the cotton or tobacco fields. The menhaden chanteys migrated to

Lewes in the 1920s with the African American labor force and continued until the last factory closed. The coordinated movement of the crews enhanced the strength of each individual as they pulled together in unison.[16]

For example, one song reflects the desire to return to Virginia or North Carolina.

Chanteyman:
I left my baby standin' in the back door cryin'
Honey, don't go!

Fishermen:
Lord, Lord, don't go!

Chanteyman:
I'd go home, but ain't got no money!

Fishermen:
Lord, Lord, ain't got no money!

Chanteyman:
Gonna row here a few days longer.
Then I'm goin' back home!

Fishermen:
Lord, Lord, goin' back home![17]

Another chantey echoed a solidarity among the laborers. In the song, Weldon refers to a large lumber mill in North Carolina.

Chanteyman:
Captain, if you fire me, fire me.

Fishermen:
Fire, fire me!

Chanteyman:
You got to fire my buddies too.

Fishermen:
Fire my buddies! Fire my buddies!

Chanteyman:
We will catch a load
And get back to Weldon on the road.

Fishermen:
On the road! On the road!

Chanteyman:
I am going back to Weldon
To get a job in the Weldon yard!

Fishermen:

The Weldon yard! The Weldon yard![18]

Some songs hit a bawdy note as the end of this one shows.

Chanteyman:
I have a girl in Baltimore!
Hey, hey, honey!

Fishermen:
Hey, hey, honey! Hey, hey, honey!

Chanteyman:
She's long and she's tall.

Fishermen
Hey, hey, honey! Long and tall!

Chanteyman:
Streetcar runs right by her door!
Hey, hey, honey!

Fishermen:
Hey, hey, honey! By her door! [19]

These songs helped form the cohesive unit that tightened the bunt. Once the bunt was as dense as it could get, the fish were loaded onto the ship and into the hold. Originally, a big brailling net or "dip net" was lowered into the bunt and swung on board. In the 1950s, suction hoses replaced bailing nets and sucked the hapless menhaden into the hold. After stowing the fish, the purse net was neatly replaced on the purse boats, which were returned to their davits. The captain, first mate, and crew would then sail in search of another school of menhaden until the sun began to set. The ship would sail to the fish factory ladened with hundreds of pounds of menhaden.[20]

The twenty-plus companies that owned fish plants on the Lewes beach in the nineteenth and twentieth centuries had one of two business types. The first was to operate only the factories, processing menhaden caught by ships owned by another company or individual. In the second, the company owned both the factory and vessels. The line blurred sometimes when a factory with its own ships also bought and reduced fish caught by someone else. Sometimes a company would move from one model to the other. For example, one company that operated factories in Lewes for thirty years initially had its own fleet but, as the fleet aged, the owners opted not to replace the ships and to rely on others to haul in their fish.

Every menhaden factory had a pier, usually a quarter- or a third-of-a-mile long, allowing for the returning fishing vessels to dock. As soon as possible, fishing steamers off-loaded tens of thousands of fish, some of which had already started to decompose. Because rotting lowers the quality of the fish oil collected, processing began as soon as possible to reduce spoilage. In the nineteenth century, the menhaden were removed from the ship in tubs with a capacity of only 500 fish. The workers filled the tubs by hand and raised them by block and tackle. This labor-intensive unloading process was replaced with an elevator that lowered a large net into the hold. The "fish gang" of four or more workers shoveled the fish into a net for the elevator to lift it to the pier. Shoveling fish from the hold was replaced in the late 1940s with a vacuum that sucked the fish onto the pier and into a raw box. Once they got it into the factory, nineteenth-century operators boiled the fish in a large vat and hydraulically pressed the oil from the cooked fish. The residuum of the fish would be thoroughly mixed with sulfuric acid and placed in heaps. Alternatively, the carrion would be left in the sun for days and manually turned over to accelerate the process. This changed to coal-fired dryers that moved the fish through on a conveyor. These were replaced by more powerful dryers, also coal powered, that had rotating bins like a clothes dryer to remove the remaining water. The thoroughly dehydrated carcasses were called "fish scrap."[21]

As soon as the fish were unloaded, the watermen removed the seine nets from the purse boats to dry them. In the nineteenth century, the nets were spread out on the beach overnight for use the next morning. In the early twentieth century beach drying was replaced by "net reels." These were circular structures about 20 feet in diameter that turned on a center axle; the nets were strung on these wheels and rotated by manpower. According to Robert Orr's recollection, "[T]he men had set stations inside the wheel — there were four parallel internal walkways — and had to walk the planks without going anywhere, much the way a pet hamster uses the exercise wheel in its cage. Twelve or more men walked inside the reel at a time, at least three of the men in single file to a walkway." This was a dreadful job since the laborers inside the reel were rained on by the rotating net above with sea water pungent with fish oils and bits of decaying menhaden. To make the task endurable and to keep in rhythm as they walked, the men sang their sea chanteys.[22]

While the nets dried, the fish were moved to the factory for processing, which became known in the twentieth century as "wet-rendering." From the raw box, the fish moved along a conveyor belt though a steam cooker until the menhaden were thoroughly cooked to the point that flesh fell apart releasing the oil. After cooking, oil was pressed from the fish by either hydraulic or screw presses separating the liquid from the solid portions. Over time menhaden processing equipment used centrifugal force to separate the oil from the "press liquor" produced by the presses. The oil was cleaned and sold as "crude menhaden fish oil." After these processes removed as much oil as they could, the liquid that remained was referred to as "stick water," consisting of water and water-soluble solids. The Lewes factories at first poured 300 barrels of refuse liquid into the Delaware Bay daily. Later, they would pour the muck into "ponds" for it to evaporate in the sun or to be absorbed by the bayfront sand. To utilize the stick water, evaporators reduced the liquid into a concentrated thick syrup called "fish solubles." This was a distinct product that is high in water-soluble vitamins and minute fish remnants, which was sold for use in swine or poultry feed. By the time the captain and his crew arrived for another day searching for schools of menhaden, their previous catch was fish scrap awaiting its turn for the grinder to pulverize it into fish meal.[23]

Chapter 3

Black and White Work Side-By-Side

From World War I until the last factories closed in 1966, African American labor fueled the menhaden industry in Lewes and made the town the leading fishing port in the country. Yet the predominately African American workforce in the Lewes menhaden industry did not begin until the 1920s. Prior to World War I, brokers from Baltimore and elsewhere recruited Portuguese, German, Irish, Polish, and Norwegian immigrants as workers. In the aftermath of World War I and the curtailment of immigration, however, the Lewes labor force began primarily to rely on African American migrants from the Northern Neck of Virginia around Reedville and from coastal North Carolina. As David Cecelski, a historian of African Americans in North Carolina, explained, "Since the turn of the century, the labor for the United States fish meal and oil industry has largely been comprised of North Carolina and Virginia natives who fish out of ports between New Jersey and Louisiana."[24] This would include Delaware.

Most Black menhaden fishermen in Lewes were migrant workers for the six-month menhaden fishing season that extended from May to October. During the winter, the company owners had hired their ship captains who, in turn, began assembling their predominantly African American crews. In most cases, the captains, their crews, and their ships were carried over from year to year with few changes. The continuity of the composition of a vessel's labor force inspired an *esprit de corps* and fostered a mutual respect among the fishermen and the officers. In late April or early May, the mainly White captains and officers and a few African American watermen men made their way to where the ships had been docked for the winter. Before the 1950s, the winter storage for Delaware ships was in North Carolina, Virginia, and Maryland but later only in Maryland. As the spartan crews sailed their ships to Delaware, they would pick up the African American crewmen in various locations in Virginia and North Carolina. By the middle of June, these ships were around once or twice a day and he'd stop to talk to yo[u] [ev]eryone." This limited integration of the menhaden la[bor] lessen the historical truism that physical labor of an[d] African Americans fueled the economic engine power[ing] fifty years.[29]

Every factory worker received a salary. In the 1930s, a laborer earned $20 for thirty days work in addition to room and board – not bad pay during the Depression. By 1960, menhaden factory workers were earning $1.40 an hour or about $225 for thirty days work. Five dollars were held back, called "hold pay," to ensure that the men would stay the entire season. The boats used a "share" system that reflected a model that had developed in the whaling industry. Except for the captain, who received a negotiated price for each thousand menhaden landed, every crewman from the mate to the deckhand received a weekly salary plus bonus for each thousand fish or "share." Both the salary and share reflected the ship's hierarchy of deckhand, cook, engineer, pilot, and mate. As one went up in the hierarchy, he received a larger salary and a greater amount for every thousand fish. In 1912, the income ranged from a crewman's $35 to $45 monthly wage and 1 or 1.5 half cents for every thousand caught to that of a mate's $50 to $100 monthly wage and bonus of 12.5 to 18.5 cents for every thousand fish. For all but the captain, a "hold pay" and a "grub" bill were deducted from each paycheck. Important for the watermen, the money for a share of the catch increased with the price of menhaden. The price for a gallon of menhaden in 1931 was 15 cents; the price in 1956 was $180. While the African American seamen netted good money during the seasons in the 1950s, the Black Lewestowners still took temporary jobs during the other months in oyster fishing, in the Doxie clam factory, in the Diamond State Poultry plant, or in odd jobs as laborers.[30]

Since the factories were two miles from the town of Lewes and the days long, the companies provided housing and meals for workers. The factory workers lived in segregated bunk houses, where fishermen sometimes slept, while primitive sleeping accommodations were also available aboard the boats for the crew. The mess halls provided three meals a day for the factory workers and, although the ship crews occasionally ate a meal ashore, most of their meals were aboard the vessel. The cooks in the ship gallies were African American men and in the mess halls ashore White women. As the manager of a menhaden plant

…where described it, "We provide our plant employees with eating facilities. We maintain four bunk houses for the colored workers. Another brick building is set aside to house the White folks on the factory payroll."[31]

Initially, the rural Black wives of fishermen generally stayed by themselves at home in the South for six months a year. They had to manage the households independently, from finances to home maintenance to raising the children. Most wives also had part-time jobs, such as housekeeping and eldercare for White families or picking crabs and shucking oysters at nearby factories. Many White wives of the captains, officers, and senior personnel also initially remained in Virginia or North Carolina to manage the family. Some of the wives of captains and other senior officials, however, would follow their husbands to Lewes for the summer months. They left after the school term ended for the children and returned before the school term started. As the wife of a bookkeeper later recounted,

> . . . the trips that we had to make -- every summer, you know, to leave our home and our friends . . . when we were going to New Jersey and Delaware. . . . We didn't actually know where we were going to live for those three months. And who our neighbors were going to be. So, in a way it was exciting and in a way you dreaded it.

Whether being the head of the house in North Carolina or Virginia or driving alone up and down the East Coast, the menhaden industry produced strong and independent women.[32]

Not unusual for an industrial economy based on unskilled migrant laborers was a continual presence of street crime and property crime. A common complaint against the fish plants was the "class" of their employees. As early as 1900, crime caused the town to hire a policeman to be on duty Saturdays during the menhaden season. About a decade later, as crime increased, this part-time policing was expanded to a year-round, everyday position, formally establishing the police department.[33]

A report of a street robbery of an African American factory worker prompted the *Delaware Coast News* to editorialize, "Hold ups and petty robberies in Lewes are getting in style. . . . Four robberies within in the last two months, one car stolen and about six hold-up performances on the beach is a record we should not be proud of." The Lewes beach front was the center for much of the crime. A local resident pleaded with the commissioners to have a police officer patrol the area for protection "from the lawless element on the beach." A section of the beach to the west of the fish plants earned the nickname "Hell's Kitchen," and the press urged, "Something must be done in order that Lewes might not become the laughingstock of the whole state." Weekly disorderly conduct occurrences on the beach culminated with a shooting after a fight in Hell's Kitchen. Crime thus became a major issue in the 1930 mayoral election. In response, the town commissioners throughout the 1930s appointed special police officers and assigned additional work to the permanent officers starting in June until the "closing of the fish factories" for the season.[34]

Despite the pollution and crime, the benefits to the Lewes economy were undeniable. Even before the arrival of the first fish factory, maritime businesses had always been the spark plugs for the Lewes economy. In the nineteenth century, sailing vessels from around the world heading to and from the port of Philadelphia reported to Lewes for instructions. Such orders had been transmitted via telegraph for the many agents of foreign shipping companies who lived in Lewes. While in port, ships would provision and sailors would take liberty, boosting the local economy. With the widespread use of the wireless radio in the 1920s, ships received commands while at sea and had no need to stop in Lewes. Shipping of agricultural products from Lewes to New York and Philadelphia declined as the railroad assumed dominance in the nineteenth century, becoming virtually non-existent after World War I. When canned vegetables from the Eastern Shore were shipped from Lewes to New England in 1939, it was front page news, "recalling . . . the days when Lewes could boast of its place as a commercial port." Menhaden commercial fishing filled the maritime void left by the sailing ships.[35]

With the resurrection of the menhaden businesses after World War I, the payroll rose from 600 to 800 workers in the factories, on the fishing steamers and in administrative positions. Most of these employees were in Lewes only during the fishing season and lived in bunk houses near the factories and piers. By the 1950s, the number of workers rose to over 1,000, again an overwhelming majority of the seamen and laborers being African American. Yet with a population of 1,923 in 1930 and 2,904 in 1950, the fishing companies' payroll was a major part of the Lewes economy. In addition to the infusion of payroll cash into Lewes, local businesses also provided support services to the fisheries. A constant source of revenue into the town became known as "grubbing them fishboats," or providing provisions to ships and to the dining halls near the factories. Selling supplies extended to providing a variety of other goods and services. When capital improvements or repairs were needed to the physical plants, the fish factories employed local help, thereby expanding the economic impact. Repairs were frequent, such as when the winter ice floes or nor'easters would damage or destroy the fisheries' piers and buildings. To expedite repairs or routine maintenance, the fisheries relied on local craftsmen. Twice, in 1926 and 1934, the fish factories suffered major fires. The latter fire consumed the vacant buildings initially erected two decades earlier. The factory was rebuilt from the burnt ruins into one of largest plants in the country utilizing local labor and materials.[36]

Following World War II, the menhaden factories laid the foundation for the spectacular success of the industry in 1950s. In short order, menhaden operations were soon surpassing their pre-war standards relying on local labor. For example, Fish Products Company invested heavily in capital improvements, nearly $1 million in 1947. The following year, it spent over $1.6 million, including an all-concrete silo for fish meal whose footprint was nearly 5,000 sq. feet and towered 140 feet high. This structure dominated the Lewes beachfront from all directions. But most of the capital improvements went toward machinery for the factory and the ships. In November 1948, the Fish Products president boasted:

> We have a new office, and practically a new factory. We have rebuilt the entire factory.... [I]t is entirely different from what it was [during the war] . . . Naturally with improvements we use very few men compared to the number we used [during the war], . . . and we of course have a much more efficient operation.[37]

With the growth of this labor-intensive industry during the 1950s, its local impact only increased: menhaden fisheries became *the* major engine driving the Lewes economy. If Lewes was where menhaden was king, it was Black watermen and factory workers who made the crown.

CHAPTER 4

The Menhaden Industry in Lewes Begins

Before the Civil War, the menhaden national enterprise, or fishery, was based out of New England and Long Island. Immediately after the war, a menhaden fisherman from Maine, Elijah Reed, saw that competitive fishing in his home state reduced his catches and sought a more plentiful fishery. This led him to the Chesapeake Bay, where he established a factory in Virginia's Northumberland County on the Northern Neck in the town that bears his name today, Reedville. Fifteen years later, over sixty factories dotted the Atlantic coast from the Carolinas to Maine, each relying on steam-powered vessels and located on or near the coast but somewhat protected from the sea. However, no factory existed between the mouth of the Chesapeake and northern New Jersey. To fill this void, veteran owners of functioning menhaden plants elsewhere looked for a location in that area. A site for a factory needed to be close to the fishing grounds in the Atlantic yet fairly insulated from oceanic storms. Also important was that it had to be at least a mile away from a major population center that would object to the obnoxious odors from rotting fish and to the pollution of nearby waters. Lewes fit the bill. The bayfront inside Cape Henlopen between the Delaware Bay and the Atlantic Ocean offered a shore for factories protected from the direct onslaught of ocean storms yet with direct access to the deep ship's channel at the entrance to the Delaware Bay. As a bonus, it was relatively uninhabited and two miles from the population center of Lewes.[38]

The town of Lewes controlled the beaches of the Delaware Bay through a grant from William Penn in the seventeenth century. In 1883, John Luce and Edward C. Luce, owners of fish factories in Connecticut, asked the Lewes town commissioners for a lease to build a "fish mill." Six weeks after the Luce Brothers' lease was signed, the town agreed to a lease with a second Connecticut-based menhaden company, Samuel S. Brown & Co., for land adjoining the Luce Brothers to the east. Since

Samuel S. Brown's partner was James Lennen, the ownership of the fish plant was sometimes referred to as Brown & Lennen. Both companies started up their processing factories and operated them for the next fifteen years. In 1897, the town commissioners signed a third lease. This one was with Albert Morris of Northumberland County, Virginia, for land next to Brown & Lennon on the east, where he would build his Delaware Fish Oil and Fertilizer Co.* Two months later, newspapers reported that Morris' construction was progressing so quickly that they should be ready by the season, just three months away. Since all three companies were started by men outside of the Lewes area and of Delaware, Lewestowners would soon refer to them as "foreign companies."[39]

Before signing a lease with the two Connecticut firms, Lewes commissioners knew about the loathsome side effects of menhaden processing and did not enter into these agreements naively, nor were they unaware that fish processing factories spawned pollutants. Before the approval of the bayfront lease to the Luce Brothers, more than two miles from the town, the commissioners had checked with other municipalities that permitted menhaden plants in their jurisdictions. In response, they received letters "from New London, Mystic, and Chincataque [sic] saying Fish Mills were not injurious to health and were not complained about in regard to smell when one mile or more away." Such would not be the case in Lewes, however. In just their third year of operation, the Luce Brothers were criminally indicted by the state for operating and maintaining a common or public nuisance. The jury, however, concluded that not enough people were directly affected by rank odors to merit a guilty verdict.[40]

A more serious legal challenge came in 1889, immediately after the United States government had established a quarantine station just one-half mile to the east of the factories. All passenger liners destined for Philadelphia had to stop in Lewes so federal health officials could examine each passenger. They would quarantine any immigrant in ill-health at the station, which was in the path of the prevailing winds carrying the smell of dead fish. The United States government filed civil suit in state courts against the factory owners to force the plants to close. Witnesses, under oath, overwhelmingly supported the plaintiff's

---

*Thomas F. Price of Long Island, New York and his brother, jointly known as the Price Brothers, may also have been involved in this third plant. See Judith Atkins Roberts, "The Menhaden Industry in Lewes," *Journal of the Lewes Historical Society*, 3, 37.

"contention as to the nauseating, discomforting or disagreeable and nauseating odors." One likened it to "a rotten egg when it is broken." The stench of decaying fish affected the employees and the passengers quarantined at the facility to such an extent as to cause vomiting and other physical ailments. Equally pervasive in the depositions were vivid complaints about the large green flies from the putrefying fish or from evaporating pools of stick water: "They were literally in swarms . . . so thick that they [on window screens] would cut off of the view through the windows" and "really darken the room" despite the summer sun. Inevitably, the flies would invade buildings so that "it was impossible to leave food exposed at all, even a short period of time." Another swore that his "dinner table [was] fearfully full of flies."

Yet no specific illness or disease could be traced to the rank smells and hordes of green flies. William P. Orr Jr., a physician who would become president of a fish factory decades later, tried to do so. He argued that some residents, including "quite a number of them around Lewes," were so annoyed by and so worried about the smell that their physical health was injured: "They believe that it affects their health, and they worry, and it produces, or causes, I must say, I think an injury to their health. . . . I do not think that the odor is injurious, but I think that there are people who are affected by it simply because they are annoyed so much by it." After nearly sixteen years of litigation, a judge ordered the processing plants to install deodorizing equipment and to stop polluting the bay. The federal government's legal effort to close the factories had failed.[41]

The case was probably moot anyway because the three original foreign companies were all replaced by a single foreign conglomerate. New Jersey investors incorporated the American Fisheries Company in 1898. The new enterprise had purchased a British patent for cooking menhaden, for extracting oil, and for drying fish carcasses because of the claim that it was 30 percent more efficient than earlier processes. It also acquired seventeen plants, including three in Lewes, and the associated fishing steamers in seven states. Within two years, American Fisheries Company had moved machinery from four plants to the remaining twelve, including those in Lewes. Thirty steam ships were devoted exclusively to menhaden fishing with a state-of the-art repair facility in Rhode Island. One contemporary commentator wrote, "With this event the movement toward consolidation reached its dramatic conclusion. . . . The new company abolished competition." The three factories in Lewes were the southern lynchpin of what was popularly known as the "Menhaden Trust." This kind of corporate structure was common in the late 1800s in other industries, such as oil, steel, and banking.[42]

But the British patents for new ways to cook and process the fish were not as profitable as anticipated, and the American Fisheries Company went into voluntary receivership in March 1900. The receivers arranged for a reorganization of the assets, including the Lewes factories, into the United States Menhaden Oil and Guano Company, incorporated a month later. This new company existed for only three months. Yet another concern, the Fisheries Company, was incorporated in July and acquired all property and rights to the nascent United States Menhaden Oil and Guano Company. Within just four months, the American Fisheries Company and its Menhaden Trust had become the Fisheries Company. Given the short life of the U.S. Menhaden Oil and Guano Company and a similarity in names between the American Fisheries Company and the Fisheries Company, the process was essentially a reorganization of the American Fisheries but without the British patents.[43]

In March 1906, Joseph Wharton of Philadelphia purchased controlling interest in the Menhaden Trust and its Lewes factories. He owned Bethlehem Steel and had the moniker "Nickel King" because he started refining that metal in the United States, although he is probably best remembered for endowing the Wharton School of Business at the University of Pennsylvania. In the next year, three disasters struck – a dismal fishing season, destruction of the trust's factory on Long Island, and the Panic of 1907. As a result, Wharton's Fisheries Company declared bankruptcy in October 1907. The *Philadelphia Inquirer* reported, "Bankers and brokers found it hard to understand how a concern of the wealth, influence, and standing of the Fisheries Company should have come to so disastrous end."[44]

The trust, which had lasted from 1898 to 1907, fractured into several regional corporations. In New Jersey and Delaware, the operation was called the Menhaden Fishing Company. At the end of its third season, in 1910, a fire destroyed two of its three factories in Lewes. After this loss, the company gave up on land-based factories and changed its business model. In the place of plants, the company started to raise capital to purchase a large steamer to operate as a floating factory. This massive ship would follow the annual migration of the menhaden up the Atlantic coast in the spring and down in fall. This would enable nearly year-round fishing instead of a limited season that land plants dictated. The floating fish oil factory would become an investment of $1 million with three generators, equipped with 750,000-gallon tanks for fish oil and a daily capacity to process 10,000 barrels of menhaden. With its corporate strategy shifting away from land-based factories, the Menhaden Fishing Company did not rebuild the Lewes factories. This left the Lewes bayfront in 1911 with only one fish plant.[45]

To fill this vacuum, local businessmen saw an opportunity for them to own factories. Lewestowners began to refer to these as "home companies" and liked that the profits would remain in Lewes. One stock prospectus for such a "home fish factory" claimed, "Foreigners have come and carried off the fortunes from their investments and it was only recently that the home people awoke to the realization that they could command this business and these fortunes themselves." The first effort to tap into this sentiment for local ownership occurred in 1911, when the commissioners of Lewes awarded a highly favorable lease to the newly incorporated Lewes Fisheries Company, a Delaware corporation. The lease ceded use of 1,500 feet of bayfront property for the factory to manufacture fish oils and fertilizers for a token rent of $1.00 per year for ten years. Lewes business owners and bankers met and raised over $13,000 to build a home fish factory on the leased land. The seven men selected to lead the fledgling company would ultimately become involved with all home companies processing menhaden: William C. Lofland, David Burbage, William H. Bookhammer, John R. Baylis, James T. Lank, Harland M. Joseph, and William J. Thompson. From these, Lofland became president of the corporation. The press gushed that "everybody is backing this local industry and are subscribing stock." The *Delaware Pilot* optimistically forecasted, "There does'nt [sic] seem to be a risk in the affair, for if out of town capitalists can make one go, our town people should be able to a make a success of it." The newspaper's analysis oozed local confidence:

> The only way that it can be a failure is by mismanagement and judging from the Board of Directors elected, this will not be done, so if you are able to take stock don't fail to get it at once, as it will be a money maker for you and will assist a home concern to make a permanent manufacturing plant here, which is bound to leave

many thousands of dollars in the town.

Its conclusion was obvious: "Everyone will feel this either directly or indirectly, so help to push this home factory along." For the 1911 season, the Lewes bayfront had two fish companies with each operating a factory, the New Jersey-based Menhaden Fishing Company and the Lewes-based Lewes Fisheries Company.[46]

With the business operations of the Menhaden Fishing Company moving from land-based factories to floating factories, its remaining land-based factory in Lewes was ready for a friendly take-over. Three prominent Lewestowners incorporated the Delaware Fish Oil Company to buy it. This became a reality when the Lewes commissioners approved assignment of the Menhaden Fishing Company lease, including its pier and every building, to the new corporation. Its subscribers were Thomas R. Ingram, William P. Orr Jr., and Ebe W. Tunnell, a former governor of Delaware. Tunnell soon faded from the company, but seven men from Lewes joined the board of directors.* These included Lewes Mayor James T. Thompson, who was also named the president and the general manager of the company. In 1912, the two Lewes menhaden operations were "home" factories.[47]

Mayor Thompson was first elected in 1900. He was born on a Sussex County farm in 1843, attended the local public schools, and graduated from the University of Pennsylvania with a medical degree. After he practiced medicine for six years in western Sussex County, he gave up life as a physician and began a career in business. After co-owning retail establishments in Lewes and owning hotels in Rehoboth Beach, he acquired the Delaware House Hotel in Philadelphia. He amassed a small fortune, moved full time to Lewes, and retired in 1896. Four years later, he was elected to his first of twenty-nine one-year terms as mayor, making him Lewes' longest serving town executive, though the terms were not consecutive. Twice, he chose not to run for reelection, yet won the next election. He declined to run in 1913, the first mayoral election after he became president and general manager of the Delaware Fish Oil Company. It is not known what role, if any, his position with a company owning land from the town played in his decision not to seek reelection. Again in 1926, Thompson opted not to seek reelection for an

---

*Harry C. Maull, William Maull, Lewes W. Mustard, L. Finley Ross, John M. Vessels, and James T. Thompson. When William Maull died in 1915, Edgard W. Ingram took his place on the board.

unknown reason. When Thompson died at the age of eighty-six in 1930, he was thought to be the oldest of any current mayor in the country.[48]

One year after the start of the Delaware Fish Oil Company in 1912, the third home company was established when five entrepreneurs filed incorporation papers for the Coast Fish Oil and Fertilizer Company. Officially, the original subscribers were Edgar M. Baylis, Harry Hankin, Fred G. Myers, William A. Russell, and Elmer Outten. While the first four were from Lewes, the last was not. Elmer Outten had been a prominent businessman and civic leader in Lewes but abruptly relocated to Dover. When the story about the fish company appeared in the local newspapers, his name was not included as a subscriber. Outten's residence might contradict the statement in the stock prospectus promoting "the corporation's organization – *entirely* by home people" [emphasis in original]. Its president was David W. Burbage, a member of the original group that William C. Lofland had led to launch the Lewes Fisheries Company two years earlier.[49]

Fish factories need vessels. The Lewes Fisheries Company purchased the four-year-old *Breakwater* for its first season. During the next two years, the firm built the *City of Lewes*, the *Rehoboth*, and the *Henlopen*. Before building the *Delaware* and the *Sussex*, the Delaware Fish Oil Company initially acquired two thirty-year-old boats, the *Fearless* and the *Albert Brown*. The third home company, Coast Fish Oil and Fertilizer Company, owned the *Mary B. Garner* and the *David W. Burbage*, which were constructed by a well-known Delaware shipbuilding firm in Milford, William G. Abbott and Company. The company's promotional materials bragged, "As this is a Delaware Company to promote the interests of Delaware, this boat will be built in Delaware."[50]

While Lewes' three home companies, each with one factory, were firmly established on the eve of World War I, they did not occupy all the bayfront property. On the east side of Coast Fish Oil and Fertilizer, 500 feet lay empty up to the area where the United States had built an iron pier for shipping interests, known simply as the "Iron Pier" on the U.S. Government Reservation.[51]

Although this bayfront parcel lacked a menhaden plant, it was not fully vacant; in fact, several people resided there. One of these was Katherine Lane Anderson. In 1900, she acquired the lot immediately adjacent to the pier. Katherine Lane Anderson probably was the legal name of Lillian Lawrence, who was known as "Miss Lil," the operator of the "house of ill repute" near the pier. Survey maps at the time labeled the parcel as that of "Mrs. Lillian Lawrence." In 1911, the transfer documents identified the seller as "Katherine Anderson formerly Katie Lane." The *Philadelphia Inquirer* reported that this Iron Pier property "owned by Miss Lawrence, had been sold to a fish factory concern." Katherine Lane Anderson, operator of Miss Lil's brothel, apparently sold the plot in April 1917 to Harvey Sickler from New York and his Neptune Fishing Company.[52]

Despite legal requirements, many inhabitants, including Anderson, never obtained a formal lease or the needed permits. Still, the tenants paid annual fees to the town for the use of the land. Sickler claimed that Lawrence had a *de facto* ownership of the land because she and the person who sold her the land had resided there for nearly fifty years, made improvements, and paid rent the entire time. Statutorily, however, the occupants were still squatters. Another legal issue was that Neptune Fishing Company argued that it had bought the entire 500-foot strip and that another fish oil company would claim that it had a lease for 400 feet of the 500 feet but never built on it. Neptune Fishing Company's ability to use the 500-foot parcel of bayfront property was in legal limbo.[53]

Upon learning that this company owned by a New Yorker would be erecting another factory, the representatives of the three home factories vigorously objected to the competition. Their first line of attack was the pier in the Delaware Bay that the new company would need for its ships to unload their catch. With responsibility to ensure that the Delaware Bay remained navigable, only the U. S. Army Corps of Engineers could authorize construction of the pier. To thwart the project, Thomas R. Ingram, an officer of the year-old Delaware Fish Oil Company, wrote his senator in Washington, D.C., asking for the senator's help with the Corps of Engineers to prevent the construction of the pier and thus to preserve the navigable waters. Such edifices, Ingram argued, could increase shoaling by changing the bay's currents, which would add more sand to the sandbars in the inner harbor and impede navigation to the extant piers. He summarized the impact: "We would simply be put out of business, which means that the people of this town and Sussex County who have put their money in these home industries would have to submit to outsiders with no state interest whatever coming in and riding slip shod over home people."[54]

The Army Corps of Engineers announced a public hearing to consider the application of the Neptune Fishing Company to construct its pier. On a cold but sunny day in February 1912, more than forty people from Lewes journeyed to Philadelphia for the session, which quickly devolved into an argument over legal title to the bayfront plot. The attorneys for Neptune Fishing Company argued that it had purchased 500 feet of waterfront property from Katherine Anderson, identified in the newspapers as "Miss Kate Lane," née Lawrence. The Town of Lewes questioned Anderson's right to sell, and the Coast Fish Oil and Fertilizer Company claimed rights to 400 feet of it. The attorney representing Lewes then "claimed the remaining 100 feet for the town of Lewes on the grounds that Miss Lane had only occupied it as a squatter." The Corps of Engineers summarized the evidence: "opposition to the erection of the structure . . . [is] based however not upon anything likely to interfere . . . [with navigation]. Since the evidence presented at the hearing shows that the title to the site of the proposed dock is in dispute, the Secretary declines to grant a formal permit for the structure but interpose no objection to its construction. . . ." A newspaper's earlier prophecy that "the matter will have to be taken to the courts for adjustment" was reinforced by the Corps of Engineers' assertion that "the question of ownership of the site must be settled by the local courts."[55]

This effort by an outsider to build another fish plant ended in a legal quagmire. The next year, in 1913, Neptune Fishing Company admitted that the legal hurdles were too high and sold whatever bayfront interest it had to the Atlantic Phosphate Company, another New York corporation. The new owners went into receivership the next year, and the receiver sold the Lewes rights to the Hydraulic Phosphate Company, a Tennessee corporation which, in an unlikely twist, sold its interests back to the former owner, "Katherine Anderson (former Katie Lane)." This pre-war effort by a New Yorker to erect a foreign factory in Lewes had come to naught and left only the three home factories in Lewes. Each had a prominent Lewestowner as its president: Lewes Fisheries Company under William C. Lofland; Delaware Fish Oil Company under Mayor James T. Thompson; and Coast Fish Oil and Fertilizer Company under David W. Burbage.[56]

CHAPTER 5

A Tale of Two Home Companies

The United States' entry into World War I in April 1917 changed the menhaden industry in Lewes. Its ships with tall masts holdings crow's nests high aloft were prized by the military for oceangoing reconnaissance work, and the government soon requisitioned some of the vessels owned by the Lewes companies for laying mines and patrolling for submarines as part of the military efforts to protect shipping. Concerned that a lack of ships would cause a shortage of fish meal, a fertilizer trader in Baltimore exaggerated the situation within days of the declaration of war: "Our [fertilizer] industry will suffer seriously due to the lack of raw materials. The menhaden fish industry has already discontinued as the government has [seized] . . . the fishing vessels for naval purposes." Even though "discontinued" is an exaggeration, the government's need for menhaden fishing vessels transformed each company, beginning with Coast Fish Oil and Fertilizer Company and the Delaware Fish Oil Company.[57]

The Coast Fish Oil and Fertilizer Company had already sold its two-year-old *David W. Burbage* to the government and within weeks of the declaration of war sold its remaining steamer, the *Mary B. Garner*. The company also leased its property, pier, and buildings on the bay to the government for use as a naval base to supply ships with crew, ordnance, and food. With neither boats nor a factory, the Coast Fish Oil and Fertilizer Company existed on paper only, its sole source of income from the lease of its assets to the U.S. Navy.

As the war was winding down in late 1918, the government returned the factory, whose owners had to decide whether to resume operations or to sell its plant. At a stockholder meeting in Lewes, a majority voted to resume fishing and hired Joseph E. Virden to be its superintendent, a veteran of the menhaden industry in Lewes. Not interested in buying ships to replace the vessels sold two years earlier, Virden arranged for two companies to provide steamers and crews to bring the menhaden into its factory: Virginia Fisheries Company; and Seminole Fertilizer and Oil Company with its *Seminole, Samuel Brown,* and *Caroline Vineyard*.[58]

Reflective of the labor trouble in postwar America, worker unrest confronted Coast Fish Oil and Fertilizer Company. At the height of the 1919 season, the crew abruptly walked away from one of the vessels under contract, *Samuel Brown*, leaving it tied up at the pier for several days awaiting a replacement crew. At the end of the season, the same steamer saw its entire crew leave again. At the factory itself, the labor force struck in November for an increase in wages from $3 to $5 a day. Rather than concede to these demands, management found new employees to replace the strikers. Thus, Coast Fish Oil and Fertilizer Company operating a factory with menhaden provided by other entities was not without its problems.[59]

Fifteen hundred feet to the west on the Lewes bayfront was the Delaware Fish Oil Company. Immediately after the declaration of war, the United States government had requisitioned the company's four fishing steamers—*Albert Brown*, *Delaware*, *Fearless*, and *Sussex*—and three months later its directors sold the floundering corporation at below-market value during a public auction held at the Hotel Rodney in downtown Lewes. The buyer was Albert W. Robinson, an attorney from nearby Laurel who, according to the newspapers, "claimed to represent a syndicate." This claim was true, as Robinson immediately retained one-seventh of the assets while selling the remaining six shares to the men who would become the board of the new Breakwater Fisheries Company that assumed ownership of the plant upon its incorporation. Four of the shares went to members of the board who had overseen the dissolution: Edgar W. Ingram, Lewis W. Mustard, William P. Orr Jr., and John M. Vessels. The two remaining portions of the syndicate went to Thomas C. Horsey of Dover and William H. Virden.* One member of the old company's board did not become involved with the new enterprise: Mayor James T. Thompson, who was also the president and general manager. Apparently, the four board members had engineered a bankruptcy-and-auction maneuver to remove Thompson from being an owner or manager of their company.[60]

Even before they had chartered the Breakwater Fisheries Company in August 1917, the owners leased it to Thomas Hayes and Raymond J. Anderton for the remainder of the season. Hayes and Anderton owned

---

*The *Milton Chronicle* reported that William E. Wolfe was also involved (*Milton Chronicle*, August 24, 1917); Mayor James T. Thompson also swore to Wolfe's involvement (Summary of Testimony, 55-56, Commissioners of Lewes v. Breakwater Fisheries Sussex County Chancery Court Case Files, c. 1895-1930, Misc. Cases B-D, Delaware Public Archives, Dover, Delaware).

several other menhaden plants and fishing vessels making it, according to the *Milford Chronicle*, "one of the largest of its kind doing its kind of business in America." The three-month lease gave Hayes and Anderton their first toehold in the Lewes fishery. The newspaper also predicted a bright future and claimed that both Breakwater Fisheries Company and the home-owned Coast Fish Oil and Fertilizer Company were "running at full blast and using seven fishing steamers. . . . Help is so scarce that a part of the help had to be imported from Baltimore. From all indications and reports these two factories that are in operation will have a good season, as fish seem to be very plentiful in the bay and in the ocean."[61]

The purchase of the Delaware Fish Oil Company plant by Albert W. Robinson also included the remainder of its lease with the town of Lewes. This lease, signed in 1912, covered just over 2,000 feet of bayfront land for twenty-five years. But the Delaware Fish Oil Company had never used the eastern half of the bayfront property that extended from its factory to the edge of the Coast Fish Oil and Fertilizer Company land. Three of the seven partners in the new enterprise--Thomas C. Horsey, John M. Vessels, and William H. Virden--appeared before a regular meeting of the Lewes commissioners with a deal in mind. Breakwater Fisheries Company and the Lewes commissioners agreed to a reduced payment from $1,200 per year to $300 until 1921 and then $500 annually after that in exchange for ceding back to the town the unused land.[62]

For the 1918 and 1919 seasons, the directors of the Breakwater Fisheries Company renewed the lease of the plant to Hayes and Anderton, who processed the fish caught with their own ships from elsewhere on the Atlantic Coast and by other independent boat owners primarily based in Virginia. This home-owned foreign-operated model, however, provided only a temporary solution to the "us-versus-them" controversy.[63]

Another home company had a brief excursion into ship construction. The government's demand for vessels at its entry into World War I enticed some Lewes entrepreneurs. After all, they had witnessed and experienced the sale of somewhat dilapidated boats to the government for hundreds of thousands of dollars. As a result, the Marine Operating Company was organized and emerged in November 1917 with the sole purpose of financing the construction of ships. It was, however, a misadventure in shipbuilding.

The officers of the new company were all well-known Lewestowners who had served on boards of menhaden fishing companies: L.W. Mustard, president; William H. Bookhammer, vice-president; Edgar W. Ingram, treasurer; David Burbage, secretary; and Edwin C. Marshall and William P. Orr Jr., directors.* They contracted with William G. Abbott Company of Milford to build two steamers. According to news reports, the Marine Operating Company was "building them for speculative purposes. . . . It is rumored that they will be sold to the government upon completion." As with many seafaring projects, expectations were not the realizations.

As months passed, the two proposed steamers became only one, the *John R. Baylis*. The expected delivery date in March 1918 came and went with the launch finally taking place in September. Since a land war in Europe had replaced the battle on the seas, a sale to the government was not likely. So, the Marine Operating Company sold its vessel the following spring to the Breakwater Fisheries Company. Because four men served on the boards of both companies, they were essentially selling it to themselves. This transfer would allow the use of home-owned steamers to engage in fishing even though operated by non-residents Hayes and Anderton.

Because of its new role as a fishing steamer, the *John R. Baylis* cruised from Milford to Baltimore to be outfitted with the equipment and machinery needed for fishing and with a state-of-the-art oil burning engine. Leaving Baltimore, the *John R. Baylis* stopped at Reedville, Virginia, to take on a fishing crew and arrived in Lewes in June 1919 – over two and-one-half years after construction began. Unfortunately, the *Baylis* had to tie up around three months later in Wilmington for extensive repairs to its engine and dynamo. After fishing for only one less-than-stellar season, the *John R. Baylis* was sold to a Virginia company. All in all, this home company venture into ship construction was an underwhelming success.[64]

As World War I ended, the two home companies were undergoing changes that made them dependent on people outside of Lewes. The Coast Fish Oil and Fertilizer, beset by labor difficulties, operated a factory processing menhaden provided by others; Delaware Fish Oil Company, meanwhile, was reorganized into the Breakwater Fisheries Company, whose outsider owners operated under contract.

---

*The Breakwater Fisheries Company Board of Directors in 1919 consisted of John R. Baylis, William E. Bookhammer, David W. Burbage, Thomas C. Horsey, Thomas R. Ingram, L. W. Mustard, William P. Orr, Albert W. Robinson, John M. Vessels, and William H. Virden.

Chapter 6

The Lewes Fisheries Company

From the incorporation of Lewes Fisheries Company in 1911 through the onset of World War I, its president and general manager was William C. Lofland. Born in 1860 in Milton, Delaware, Lofland owned the Hotel Henlopen in Rehoboth Beach and the Virden House in Lewes. In 1898, he moved to Wilmington and jointly owned the Hotel Wilmington for seven years. The partnership dissolved when, according to a biographical sketch of famous Delawareans in the 1920s, "Lofland became engaged in other business" and returned to Lewes. There he served as president of the Lewes Sand Company, the Lewes Canning Company, and the Lewes Gas Company. In sum, Lofland was a prominent and experienced businessman with his hand in a variety of successful interests. Yet, his involvement with the Lewes Fisheries Company would tarnish that reputation.[65]

The Lewes Fisheries Company initially operated with four fishing steamers. It first purchased the *Breakwater*. The company then built three more: the *Henlopen*, the *City of Lewes*, and the *Rehoboth*. According to Lofland, the company received "numerous inquiries" about whether it would consider selling one or more of these vessels. He reported that the board of directors would sell any or all of the steamers if a "substantial profit" would be made. Despite some negotiations between the 1916 and 1917 seasons, none resulted in a sale.

With war imminent, Lofland learned that the navy was interested in purchasing steamers and offered all four of his company's vessels to the war effort. Without publicity, the board of directors authorized the sale of the older *Breakwater* for $75,000 and each of the other three at $125,000, or a 250 percent profit. The navy brass in Philadelphia, however, were no match for Lofland's skills as a negotiator and paid $90,000 for the *Breakwater* and $150,000 for each of the newer ships, for a 300 percent profit. Naval officials in Philadelphia later admitted that they had paid too much for the steamers and were criticized by their superiors in Washington. Lofland bragged that the navy's negotiator "was the laughingstock of the whole coast."[66]

The contract required Lewes Fisheries to deliver the *Breakwater*, the *Rehoboth*, and the *City of Lewes* to the government in Philadelphia by April 20 and the *Henlopen* by May 6. The delivery date for the *Henlopen* was later because it was under contract with the navy for work in the Caribbean. Even then, the *Henlopen* did not arrive in Philadelphia until two weeks after the promised date. Embarrassed by the original contract, the navy was quick to cancel the purchase of the *Henlopen*, even though Lofland offered to sell it at a discounted price of $125,000. Lofland thus had one vessel for the 1917 season but needed two, so he purchased the *James M. Gifford*. While Lofland used both ships in his fishing operations, he simultaneously marketed them for sale. The promotions enticed a ship broker in New York to inquire on behalf of the James W. Elwell & Company for the steamer *Henlopen* but no agreement was reached.[67]

Lofland's efforts to sell the ships also attracted the attention of Robert Pennington, formerly the general counsel for The Fisheries Company, or the "Menhaden Trust," who was currently the president of a menhaden company in Florida. He visited Lofland and discussed a merger with his Lewes Fisheries Company. Such an arrangement, Pennington argued, would be mutually beneficial since the fishing seasons in Florida and Delaware occur in different months of the year, so the steamers of both companies could operate for nine months of the year. Rejecting the overture, Lofland countered that Pennington might purchase the Lewes Fisheries Company. Somewhat interested, Pennington asked for and received a statement of assets of Lofland's company.

In case Pennington might make an offer to buy the Lewes Fisheries Company, Lofland called a meeting of the board of directors. They agreed to a resolution that authorized the company president to sell the *Henlopen* and the *James M. Gifford* for $200,000. But really wanting to sell both the plant and the steamers, the board passed a second resolution that empowered the president to include the factory and the two vessels for $225,000. Any sale involving the factory needed approval from a stockholder meeting. Three days later, Lofland and James Lank, the company secretary, met with Pennington in Wilmington to discuss the sale of Lewes Fisheries Company. Lofland opened the negotiation with an asking price of $250,000 for the factory and the ships. Pennington countered with an offer for $225,000, the same amount in the directors' resolution. A $5,000 deposit sealed the contract for Pennington's acquisition of the company, its boats, its factory, and its assets – pending the approval of the stockholders. Pennington made a second offer: purchase only the two boats for $180,000, but this was less than the $200,000 in the board resolution.[68]

While negotiating, Pennington mentioned that he might need financial assistance in the purchase. Lofland volunteered to Pennington that James W. Elwell & Company was interested in buying the *Henlopen* and dangled the prospect of a quick turnaround. Pennington asked Lofland to go to New York as his representative to negotiate the sale of the vessel to Elwell. The next day, Lofland was in New York offering the *Henlopen* for $175,000. At first it was rejected. In Lofland's words, "no one could have been more surprised" than he when Elwell had an about face and agreed to buy the ship for the asking price. Elwell issued a check for 10 percent of the purchase price as down payment with the balance due upon delivery.[69]

In the agreement between Lofland and the Elwell Company for the *Henlopen*, the Lewes Fisheries Company ostensibly was the seller: it had title and issued the bill of sale through Lofland, who was its president. While Lofland claimed that the sale needed the approval of the directors, he did not mention that this would be the second time in two days he had sold the *Henlopen* and had accepted a check payable to the company.[70]

Lofland returned to Lewes and presented to a special meeting of his board of directors a letter from Pennington offering two options: (1) he would purchase just the *Henlopen* and the *James M. Giffords* for $180,000, or (2) he would buy the two steamers, the plant and all its equipment, and the unexpired term of the lease for $225,000. Pennington's letter also acknowledged that the second option was subject to stockholder approval. At the board meeting, Lofland did not disclose that the *Henlopen* was under contract to be resold to Elwell for $175,000. Without this information, the board unanimously accepted Pennington's offer to buy the entire operation and called a stockholder meeting for the following week to confirm the deal.[71]

During the week of the stockholder meeting, rumors flew through the streets of Lewes that the *Henlopen* had been sold or was being sold to the French government for $175,000. Two months earlier, the French had indeed expressed interest in purchasing the *Henlopen*. Immediately before the stockholders meeting, three board members confronted Lofland in a hallway with the rumors about the sale of the *Henlopen* to the French. With "evasive and misleading answers," according to one director, Lofland flatly denied the rumors about a sale to the French. He also attested that Pennington had sold the *Henlopen* without divulging the sum and claimed that it was all irrelevant to the matter being presented to the stockholders, namely, the sale of the Lewes Fisheries Company in its entirety for $225,000. Regarding what information was presented to stockholders, the chancellor of the Chancery Court, the chief justice of the Delaware court for corporate entity litigation, would tersely conclude, "There is a diversity of testimony on this." The stockholders did hear about and discuss reports that the *Henlopen* was likely being resold for $175,000 but were unaware of Lofland's involvement or that the buyer (Elwell) assumed he had purchased it from the Lewes Fisheries Company. When the vote was tallied, 2,317 shares were cast in favor of the sale and 148 against, much more than the two-thirds of the outstanding stock needed to adopt the resolution.[72]

On the day before the transfer of the plant and lease with the final payment, Pennington formally incorporated a fishery, the Lewes Oil and Chemical Company, owning 90 percent of the shares. The following week, Pennington transferred the assets he had acquired from the Lewes Fisheries Company to his new company. As Pennington took over the plant and its operations, Lofland assumed the day-to-day supervision of the factory and fishing boats and soon became the general manager. Pennington arranged to sell some shares in the company to Lofland and, at Lofland's suggestion, to Lewestowners James T. Lank, Harland M. Joseph, and James M. Tunnell. Lank and Joseph had served on the board of the former Lewes Fisheries Company, and Tunnell was its corporate counsel.[73]

According to Lofland, the decision to sell the Lewes Fisheries Company "was largely influenced by the losses sustained by the company during its operations during the year 1916, with losses amounting to approximately the sum of Six Thousand Dollars." He also noted that in 1917 the losses continued, "owing to a poor catch of fish and difficulties with the steamer crews." This explanation, however, is suspect. In the same declaration, Lofland pointed out that Lewes Fisheries paid a 10 percent dividend in 1917. On July 30, the Lewes Fisheries Company had between $250,000 and $300,000 in cash on hand and about $100,000 in accounts receivable. According to a Chancery Court judge, "the business was profitable from the start, dividends were declared each year." Harland M. Joseph bragged, "The Lewes Fisheries Company has been one of the most profitable if not the most profitable business venture in Sussex. . . . [The] company made large operating profits as well as large profits in the sale of its steamers." Nevertheless, Lofland, its president and general manager, had negotiated the sale of the company, represented the buyer to secure money for the purchase by selling an asset of the company in the name of the company and at an inflated price, and then resumed his position as general manager.[74]

As these intrigues publicly unraveled when summer blended into fall, one stockholder was moved to action. Charles V. Jones of Lewes sued the officers, the directors, and the company itself. Specifically, he filed a Bill of Complaint with the Court of Chancery requesting that a receiver be appointed to determine the equitable distribution of the Lewes Fisheries Company assets among its stockholders. The bill claimed that Lofland, Joseph, and Lank had committed fraud and deception in selling the *Henlopen* twice and in only arranging a pretended sale of the Lewes Fisheries Company to Pennington.

While not overtly stated in the formal filing, Jones felt that Lofland held a personal grudge against him and believed that Lofland had arranged the sale only to force Jones out and deprive him of his shares in a profitable company. Like Lofland's claim that his company was losing money, this claim of Jones is also suspect. Jones owned only nine shares or less than one-third of one percent of the outstanding stock. Bad blood had existed between the two men for at least a year after the appointment of Lofland's wife, Fredonia, as the Lewes postmistress. Jones felt that he should have been appointed to the position. Aware of this resentment, Lofland claimed that Jones filed the suit for revenge. The Lewes suit led to depositions and affidavits. When the owners of the 2,558 outstanding shares were surveyed, 1,581 of them opposed the appointment of a receiver against the owners of 1,649 shares in favor. Due to the breadth of opposition by the Lewes Fisheries stockholders and to the disagreements between Jones and his attorney, however, the Bill of Complaint was dropped and the case dismissed.[75]

For all of 1918, Lofland managed to secure ships to haul in enough menhaden for Pennington's newly organized Lewes Oil and Chemical Company. He owned the *Gifford*, which was acquired with the purchase of the Lewes Fisheries Company. He also negotiated leases with the

Neptune Fishing Company for additional ships and crews, primarily the *Cod*, the *Beckwith*, and the *Maid of the Mist*. In the middle of the following season, the Lewes Oil and Chemical Company purchased from the government the *Peter Struven* and the *Mary B. Garner* which, prior to the war, belonged to another menhaden company in Lewes. With a fleet of three vessels, the Lewes Oil and Chemical Company now had its own ships and no longer needed those of other companies. Pennington made Lofland the company's president in addition to his position as general manager. This made the Lewes Fish Oil and Chemical Company a combination of home and foreign companies, with an outsider as the principal owner but a prominent Lewestowner in charge of operations and a board of directors comprised of local businessmen.[76]

Chapter 7

More Legal Troubles for Lofland

The dismissal of the Charles V. Jones complaint in December 1917 appeared to answer the legal questions about William C. Lofland's double sale of the *Henlopen*. Not deterred, Jones persevered and continued to search for a new attorney to press the issue. In April of the following year, he met with Henry Ridgely, an attorney from Dover, who said he would investigate the situation. Ridgely "concluded the situation was hopeless." Despite that assessment, one aspect of the case worried Ridgely: the company made huge profits from selling its ships to the government for an inflated cost. The attorney was angry that someone may have "boasted of having gotten the best of the United States Government – that was a time we were in the War, and I felt indignant . . . ." Ridgely, urged by a mutual friend who intervened on Jones' behalf, agreed to investigate the case with only a guarantee that his personal expenses be reimbursed.[77]

In the summer of 1918, Ridgely filed a second Bill of Complaint alleging a series of malfeasances on the part of the Lewes Fisheries Company board of directors and asking the Chancery Court to appoint a receiver. In addition to the sales of the plant to Pennington and of the *Henlopen* to the Elwell company, Ridgely asserted several other illegal actions that went back to the beginnings of the company. Underpinning Ridgely's new claims was the understanding that the directors were to serve without compensation. Ridgely argued that each director involved with the company's incorporation received fifteen shares of stock with a par value of $100 for each share in payment for "services in organizing the company and commissions for selling the stock." During each year of the company's operation, the directors received a dividend on these shares. For each of the six years that the Lewes Fisheries Company functioned, the directors also received $1,000 annual salary. And a year after incorporation, each director "bought" seventy shares of stock with promissory notes to the company. The company books showed that the directors never made payments toward these debts other than crediting a portion of the annual dividends from shares to paying off the promissory note.

Ridgely also pointed out that Pennington had purchased the factory and steamer on August 10, when the stockholders approved the contract but did not pay for them until August 21. Therefore, Ridgely argued that the stockholders should receive the profits for the interim period between the date of the sale and the date of consummation of the transfer with payment. His final and last charge assumed that the sale of the factory and steamers had been a result of fraud. If so, the stockholders were entitled to the return or replacement of both the factory and ships.[78]

The suit named as defendants Robert Pennington, the directors individually, and the Lewes Fish Oil and Fertilizer Company.* If proved, these accusations would amount to a judgment over $400,000, according to Ridgley's calculations. Before computation of any interest, each former director would owe about $27,000 for compensation received during the company's period of operation. Robert Pennington would be obliged to pay about $68,000 for the fraud involved in the purchase of the *Henlopen* and for the profits during his interim ownership. And, if the court found that the sale of the factory and steamers to Pennington was fraudulent, the court could also order the surrender of the factory and steamers and all profits that Pennington had earned since the alleged purchase. This would add another $100,000 to $200,000 to the judgment. Against these accusations stood most of the stockholders, who were content with the dissolution of the company. Each share of the company with its par value of $100 had received $165 in dissolution dividends. This was in addition to annual dividends of 10 percent to 20 percent during the entire life of the corporation. A lawyer subsequently involved would comment: "With few exceptions, the stockholders felt entirely satisfied."[79]

After five months, the defendants filed their response to Ridgely's charges. Rather than a rebuttal, Ridgely daringly said that he would argue the case before the Chancery Court based only on the admissions in the defendants' statements and on the books of the corporation. Ridgely's strategy worked, as his oral arguments of February won the initial round. Chancery Court Chancellor Charles M. Curtis appointed

---

*The Breakwater Fisheries Company Board of Directors in 1919 consisted of John R. Baylis, William E. Bookhammer, David W. Burbage, Thomas C. Horsey, Thomas R. Ingram, L. W. Mustard, William P. Orr, Albert W. Robinson, John M. Vessels, and William H. Virden.

Joseph L. Cahall of Georgetown receiver of the Lewes Fisheries Company, with responsibility "to collect and recover the debt and property due and belonging to said company and any and all money and assets thereof unlawfully and improperly diverted from said company through any fraudulent and unlawful acts of its officers." Cahall immediately appointed as his counsel and legal advisor none other than Henry Ridgely, the very same attorney who prepared the request that a receiver be appointed.[80]

During the next few months, Cahall and Ridgely conducted a painstaking investigation into the seven years the Lewes Fisheries Company was in operation. Upon completion of the investigation, Cahall found that each director of the Lewes Fisheries Company, Robert Pennington, and the Lewes Oil and Chemical Company itself had illegally diverted funds from the company's stockholders and that each was liable for the redirected amount.[81]

Legal arguments ensued. The court first confirmed the position of the propriety of Cahall, who had been the attorney for Ridgely, serving as the receiver's counsel. The court battle then moved to determining the facts the stockholders were owed money by the defendants— each director of the Lewes Fisheries Company, Robert Pennington, and the Lewes Oil and Chemical Company itself. This required filing affidavits, taking depositions, compelling testimony from witnesses, and exchanging volleys of legal briefs. In the view of the chancellor of the Court of Chancery, this case had "testimony unusually voluminous and exhibits unusually numerous." According to Ridgely, "This was not a small case. The town was seething with this case." Cahall claimed, "The litigation was of the most onerous and exacting character. Every step was hotly contested." Reflecting upon the intense local interest in the case, diarist Lizzie Carter recorded each step of the "Fish House Trial" in her journal.[82]

During the trial, James M. Tunnel, corporate counsel of the Lewes Fish Oil and Fertilizer Company and the lead attorney representing the defendants, suggested a negotiated settlement. Ridgely opened the negotiation with a $100,000 figure. Tunnell countered with an offer of $5,000, which soon was raised to $10,000. Ridgely agreed, "if you will come over and tell us the truth." The defendants' attorney refused, and the case proceeded to final arguments before the chancellor who, in May 1921, rendered his decision. As diarist Carter wrote, "The Chancellor has given his decision on the Lewes Fish House Case. It has gone against the directors & they will have a big amt [sic] of money to pay."[83]

Indeed, the Chancery Court judge ruled that the directors had received unjustified compensation from their annual salaries, from the ninety shares awarded for organizing the company, and from the 420 shares acquired through promissory notes. The chancellor also declared that "Lofland's duplicity and breach of trust" had facilitated the sale of the *Henlopen* and therefore he and the purchaser had to repay the difference between the amount that Elwell paid for the steamer and the value the directors' resolution had assigned to the ship less broker's commission. While Pennington had to refund all the money the plant had earned between the date of purchase and the date that he surrendered the property, the court concluded that, on the claim of fraud,

> [T]he Lewes Fish Oil & Chemical Company [sic] is not entitled to any consideration as an innocent purchaser for value. It would be within the power of the court to restore in some way to the stockholders of the Lewes Fisheries Company the property [assets of the current company plus all profits since the sale] obtained from it by these unworthy methods, but at this time it does not appear to be feasible to do so.[84]

After an accounting, the six defendant directors had to return the value of 510 shares of stock they had received for "extra services" or purchased with promissory notes for a total of $96,518 plus $50,000 in interest. In other words, each defendant owed $25,253. The judgment against Pennington was $49,549. Including the $5,000 in cash the Lewes Fisheries Company had on hand when Cahall was appointed receiver, the total assets to be allotted as distribution dividends among each of the 2,345 outstanding shares amounted to $201,067.[85]

While little in the decision pleased the defendants, Pennington apparently was satisfied because he at least did not have to surrender the factory and all profits since the sale. He opted to accept the chancellor's decision and to pay his share of the judgment. The next month, October 1921, he began to extricate himself completely from the fishing industry in Lewes by transferring all assets of the Lewes Oil and Chemical Company to a new entity, Lewes Fertilizer Company. William C. Lofland, the president and general manager of Pennington's former company, assumed the same positions with the enterprise. Pennington became a director and would hold that position for two years.

If Pennington seemed to back away, his co-defendants did not. After the Chancery Court denied their request to reconsider its judgement, the director-defendants appealed. It was all for naught, as the Delaware State Supreme Court sustained the Chancellor's decision in June 1922.[86]

While the case was working its way to the Delaware's highest court, according to news reports, William C. Lofland, the lead defendant and the president and general manager of the Lewes Oil and Chemical Company, was stricken with influenza around the beginning of March 1922 and confined to his house. While he seemed to be improving and was reported to be up and about, he quickly took a turn for the worse. After falling into critical condition at Beebe Hospital, Lofland died on April 24. The obituary published in the local newspaper reported, "Mr. Lofland was stricken with influenza and grip [sic] which was followed by infection which caused his death." The official cause of death, however, was listed as "gangrene lower jaw." Due to the immediate need to prepare for the coming fishing season, the stockholders of the Lewes Oil and Chemical Company quickly selected Harland M. Joseph its general manager.[87]

To assume management of his father-in-law's businesses, including the Lewes Fertilizer Company, Lofland's son-in-law, Frank S. Carter, ended his fifteen-year career in the U.S. Navy and returned to Lewes. Apparently realizing that Joseph was well situated in his role there, Carter, with the aid of David Burbage, acquired the Menhaden Products Corporation in January 1923.* Doing no business during its first season and with Carter becoming secretary of the Lewes Fertilizer Company, the Menhaden Products Company dissolved in April 1924. In this way, Lofland's menhaden legacy continued.[88]

This legacy would suffer a second blow, however, as another legal round began in the fall when Joseph L. Cahall submitted to the Court of Chancery his "Receiver's Report and Petition for Compensation for His Services and for Allowance for his Expenses and for the Services of his Counsel." He concluded his report with a request of $20,000 for his services and of $30,000 for Ridgely, his attorney. This was despite Ridgely's initial agreement with Jones to investigate the case only for expenses. Taken together, these requests for compensation equalled about one-

---

*Two other Lewestowners were on the board of directors of the Menhaden Products Company: Robert J. Walton Jr. and Cornelius M. Eriksen.

fourth of the total amount awarded to stockholders, thereby reducing the dividend distribution from about $85.00 per share to about $65.00. The fees were based on the time expended, the complexity of the bill and, most importantly, the benefits the stockholders received solely because of their efforts. Former congressman, physician, and respected Lewestowner Hiram Rodney Burton, who owned ten shares, would have none of this. Ten days after Cahall's submission of expenses, he mailed a letter to each stockholder and urged they protest these "exorbitant and unreasonable demands." Threatened with a loss of the $20 per share, the letter described the fees as "a little less than confiscation." Burton asked that each stockholder send him a written petition asking that Cahall's expense request be slashed and promising to forward the replies to the Chancellor.[89]

As responses to his letter flowed to Burton in Lewes, Cahall's request of $50,000 compensation required additional court hearings and extended the already lengthy litigation. In early 1923, receiver Cahall and attorney Ridgely testified why their efforts justified the fees and were cross-examined by an opposing attorney. The chancellor issued a Solomonic decision to award one-half of the requested fees to the receiver and to the attorneys, or $10,000 to Cahall and $15,000 to his counsel. In the summer, each share of stock brought its owner the first distributive dividend of $60.00. In December 1924, as part of Cahall's final report, the shareholders were awarded a second and final dividend of $16.50 for each share. This was the final dissolution of the Lewes Fisheries Company that began in 1917 and ended seven and one-half years later – longer than the company itself had existed. At the end, the owner of each share of outstanding stock with a par value of $100 received a total of $241.50 in dividends – which every former director and officer of the company, including Robert Pennington, paid. This was far better than what Charles Jones could possibly have expected when he questioned the sale of the *Henlopen* and entered the world of Lofland's schemes.[90]

Chapter 8

It's in the Lease

For over twenty years, various factories had operated menhaden plants on the Lewes bayfront, but not all of it. The Lewes commissioners saw that the area still had two parcels that could support additional factories. The first was the 1,000 feet that Breakwater Fisheries had ceded back two years earlier in return for a reduction in rent and the second about 500 feet of land where Lillian Lawrence lived and which Henry Sickle sought for a plant before the war. To secure rent revenue from additional companies, the commissioners of Lewes voted in August 1917 to ask various fish companies if they were interested in leasing sites on the beach for new factories.

The Coast Fish Oil and Fertilizer Company indicated an interest in acquiring an additional 100 feet to expand its current plant, while Thomas H. Hayes and Raymond J. Anderton, who were operating the Breakwater Fisheries Company plant, also wanted an adjacent portion of the available shoreline. The town also received formal proposals from two foreign companies, the Virginia Fisheries Company and the Henlopen Fish Oil and Phosphate Company (also called the Henlopen Guano and Fish Oil Company). During a commissioners' meeting, the long-simmering home company versus foreign company conflict once again emerged. One resident claimed that "leasing sites to people with steamers . . . cripples us and renders us helpless. It brings the matter to a point where we must fight for our lives, or stand still and see our investment fade away." A Breakwater Fisheries Company director candidly admitted: "If we had known that you Commissioners was [sic] going to lease this land to foreigners we wouldn't have turned it back. We would have kept it and tried to pay the taxes." One commissioner offered an understatement, "[T]hey would rather not have foreign people build there."[91]

Despite this opposition from Lewes townsfolk, the commissioners offered to lease 300 feet of bayfront land to Henlopen Fish Oil & Phosphate Company and to Virginia Fisheries Company. One newspaper boldly headlined, "Five Factories to Operate on Lewes Beach Next

Year." The directors of the Breakwater Fisheries Company believed that the town's elected leaders defied public opinion "out of spite because Mayor Thompson wasn't in the Breakwater Fisheries Company." After all, when Breakwater Fisheries arose from the remnants of Delaware Fish Oil, Mayor James T. Thompson was one of two Delaware Fish Oil Company directors excluded from the company. Probably a stronger motivation than spite was the additional rent payments from the new leases.[92]

While Lewes was trying to lease the land to the west of Coast Fish Oil and Fertilizer Company, Thomas H. Hayes wanted possession of the bayfront to the east where the Neptune Fishing Company had tried to erect a factory in 1912. As the controversy surrounding the Neptune Fishing Company's proposal brought out, Lillian Lawrence's title to the land was somewhat clouded. While her claim was for all 500 feet along the bayfront from the Iron Pier up to the Coast Fish Oil land, she was paying rent for only 100 feet. As one attorney explained, she "had some claim to a portion of this land, at least, by reason of occupancy." Hayes' first step was to pay $2,250 to "buy out her rights," whatever they might be. He argued to the Lewes commissioners that, since he had paid a "considerable sum" to resolve her claim, he should receive a lease for only a nominal rent. Hayes then signed a sixteen-year lease for the 512 feet of land to the east of the Coast Fish Oil plant. For the first five years, the rent would be only one dollar annually and then $512 each year for the remainder of the lease.[93]

As the legal status of the beach to the east of the Coast Fish Oil and Fertilizer Company was becoming clarified, the status of land to the west became muddled. In 1912, the Delaware Fish Oil Company obtained a lease for the entire beachfront between its factory and the Coast Fish Oil and Fertilizer Company plant even though half would remain vacant. When the company was acquired by the Breakwater Fisheries Company, the lease covered the unused land. When Breakwater renegotiated its lease in late 1917, the assumption was that the annual rent would be reduced from $1,200 to $300 in exchange for surrendering back to the town the empty bayfront property.

Faced with the determination of the commissioners to lease this plot to would-be competitors of Breakwater Fisheries, one of its directors, William H. Bookhammer, met with the town's attorney, Daniel J. Layton. He wanted to see if he could leverage his friendship with Layton to persuade the attorney to use his influence with the town commissioners to keep them from leasing the bayfront lands to outsiders, Virginia Fisheries Company and the Henlopen Fish Oil Company. While Bookhammer was walking to Layton's office in Georgetown, they happened to meet each other on the street. After a brief conversation about leasing the bayfront, Bookhammer mentioned that Breakwater Fisheries had "formerly owned" the land that the town was proposing to lease. Layton did not remember a deed of surrender, so he was curious about the meaning of "formerly owned." Since they were standing in front of the Recorder of Deeds, he suggested that they go in and look up the records. When Layton reported that he could not find the crucial document, Bookhammer claimed, "Yes, it is there; I know it is one of the leases." Layton found the lease to Breakwater Fisheries Company and stopped reading at paragraph four. After rereading the paragraph, Layton blurted, "I don't see where you gave up anything." Bookhammer did not understand and, when he asked his friend to explain that remark, Layton only stated that he represented the town of Lewes, that he could not discuss it further, and that Bookhammer had better see another attorney.[94]

The paragraph in the lease that caused Layton such pause was boilerplate: "Fourth: All leases of agreements relative to the occupancy of the land and premises *hereinabove described* [emphasis added] made between the parties hereto, or their predecessors in title, are hereby cancelled and made null and void." The document had described in detail the land being leased as only the acreage on which the plant then stood and did not include the vacant 1,000 feet. Since the fourth paragraph nullified leases to the land "hereinabove described," it nullified only the land of the 1912 lease that pertained to the section that the plant occupied. The paragraph left intact the original lease as it pertained to the lands not described "hereinabove" and thus the vacant shore lands. Breakwater Fisheries Company had two legally valid leases, one from 1917 for the land on which its current plant stood and another from 1912 for the empty land between its plant and the Coast Fish Oil and Fertilizer Company.[95]

This litigious wording ended up in the document after Mayor James T. Thompson and some other commissioners had negotiated with Breakwater's general manager for the language that described the land the second lease would cover. Mayor Thompson gave the information to Thomas R. Ingram and asked him to draw up a lease. According to the mayor, Ingram was "the man who always attended to the fish house business for the town when I was concerned with the fish business." In drafting the lease, Ingram included standard language to nullify previous leases. In this case, the boilerplate language did not accurately reflect the intent of the parties to the contract. When it came time for Mayor Thompson to sign for the town, he said that he read it over and saw nothing wrong with it. Signing for the Breakwater Fisheries Company was its vice president, William P. Orr Jr., who explained that he did so only when the president, Thomas R. Horsey, was not available. When asked why he signed the lease, Orr candidly swore:

> I don't know; I was acting as vice-president of the company, and I presumed this lease was presented to me to sign; but when it was presented to me, I don't know that I read it when I signed it; I signed it as vice-president in place of Mr. Horsey, the president, and supposed the thing had been properly drawn up.

Daniel Layton, the Lewes town attorney, lamented, "[T]he Commissioners would learn sometime to employ counsel to prepare these leases, and that the whole thing was prepared by some layman who didn't know about preparing leases."[96]

The clouded legal status sank the master plan of Thomas Hayes and Raymond Anderton. According to Anderton, "We had in mind purchasing both of those plants [Breakwater and Coast Fish Oil] and arranging for extensive improvements, especially on the land not occupied. . . . Our idea was to build a fertilizer plant on this land and connect both plants so that an economical operation of them could take place." The press reported that the New York duo was proposing to triple the number of elevators to lift the fish from the boats to the plants, to erect a new pier, and to install tanks for thirty thousand barrels of fish at one time. The lynchpin for the development was a fertilizer plant on the vacant land so they could manufacture the scrap on site rather than shipping it away on barges to other plants.

The first step for Hayes and Anderton had been their acquisition of Lillian Lawrence's rights to the land east of the Coast Fish Oil and Fertilizer factory. The second step was to buy the company, which they did in January 1920. The purchase was not a difficult decision since the 1919 vote to resume operations had not been unanimous, and Hayes and Anderton were running the company anyway. The final step, and capstone to their vision, was to buy the Breakwater Fisheries Company. This assumed that any purchase would embrace both the land where the factory stood and the vacant land as well because of the "fourth paragraph." This also meant they would be leasing the bayfront from the Breakwater Fisheries Company on the west and from the Iron Pier on the east.

Despite his role as Lewes' town counsel, Daniel J. Layton represented Breakwater Fisheries in its sale to Hayes and Anderton. Almost before the ink was dry on the purchase contract, the officers of the Breakwater Fisheries Company received notification that the town had asked the Chancery Court to revise the fourth paragraph of the Breakwater Fisheries Company lease so that it would reflect the verbal agreements.[97]

The crux of the litigation went back to 1912: In question was whether three individuals who were not yet directors could ask that the company surrender 1,000 feet of bayfront land in exchange for a reduction in rent. A second question was whether Hayes and Anderton purchased the disputed land in good faith. They had opinions from attorneys stating that the documents plainly showed that Breakwater Fisheries had clear title to the land despite their knowledge that the town disputed the claim. The claim of good faith had credence since the town's attorney had represented the seller in the negotiations. In these proceedings, Daniel J. Layton had to recuse himself from serving as Lewes counsel. His younger brother, Caleb S. Layton, took on the role. After numerous briefs, hearings on motions, and three days of testimony, the Chancellor delivered his opinion in June 1922. He concluded that the lease between the Lewes commissioners and Breakwater Fisheries did not reflect the oral agreements and the mistake was a mutual one among the parties. Additionally, Hayes and Anderton were "not bona fide purchasers for value and without notice" and did not have a claim to 1,000 feet of unused land. An appeal promptly went to the State Supreme Court, which heard oral arguments in January 1923. Six months later, the court sustained the chancellor's opinion that ordered Breakwater's lease be revised so that it did not include the disputed land.[98]

Despite the litigation, the major role of Hayes and Anderton in Lewes's menhaden industry was emerging. They had operated the factories of the Breakwater Fisheries Company under lease for two years before purchasing both the Breakwater Fisheries and the Coast Fish Oil and Fertilizer Company in 1920. After their initial efforts to revamp the fish plants, one commentator prophesied, "The firm has about twenty fishing steamers, and when they all get to fishing at the two local plants, it will mean a great deal of money turned over in Lewes and should be a wonderful boon to the town." The town's coffers swelled too. Because Hayes' and Anderton's intention to operate more steamers in Lewes than during any previous season, the town expanded its water system with new wells and pumps. By supplying water to the fish factories, the town received $6,000 from the companies compared to $4,000 from its residents. A commissioner commented, "This is a source of revenue that most towns do not have." To ease the feelings against foreign fish factories in Lewes, Hayes and Anderton formed boards of directors for both companies filled with local businessmen. Indeed, four locals long associated with the menhaden business–John Baylis, William Bookhammer, Edgar Ingram, and John Vessels–were appointed to both boards.[99]

Lewes had tried to increase the number of factories on its bayfront. As proposals from potential industrialists stalled in legal disputes over whether the town had in fact additional bayfront to lease, their interest in wanting to expand into Lewes waned, possibly due to the nation's severe recession in 1920-21. The town's effort, to be sure, was unsuccessful. The episode, however, clarified the legal status of the land on both sides of the Coast Fish Oil and Fertilizer Company lease.

CHAPTER 9

There Will Be Plenty of Fish

From the 1920s to the 1950s, the names on the signs in front of the Lewes fish factories changed, as did the ownership. The profits of from each season fluctuated due to varying numbers of menhaden in the Atlantic, to abnormal weather in the Mid-Atlantic area, and to economic conditions far beyond Lewes. Coincidental with these changes, there was a long-term steadiness in the growth of the Lewes menhaden fishery that would make the town the number one fishing port in the United States.

With the resolution of the court cases arising from operations under William C. Lofland, the Lewes Fertilizer Company occupied the bayfront's western parcel. To the east, the clarification of the legal control of the land also resolved the disputed boundaries of the leases held by Thomas Hayes and Raymond Anderton; with secure leases to the land, they merged Breakwater Fisheries Company with their Coast Fish Oil and Fertilizer Company in 1924. The combination was logically named Consolidated Fisheries Company and became a single entity with two factories. The next year Anderton retired to Worcester, Massachusetts, to manage the family's textile business. He was replaced by Richard C. Hayes and John E. Hayes, brothers to Thomas. Consolidated Fisheries was thus popularly called the "Hayes Brothers factory." By 1925, only two corporations operated fish plants in Lewes: Consolidated Fisheries Company and Lewes Fertilizer Company. The former had two factories, and the latter had one.[100]

Corporate changes continued with Lewes Fertilizer Company. In the spring of 1929, it declared bankruptcy. At a sheriff's sale, both its plant and its lease were purchased by a newly formed corporation, Atlantic Fisheries Company. Six months later, a second sale sold the Lewes Fertilizer Company's steamers, and Atlantic Fisheries did not replace the vessels. Key figures in both companies were Harland Joseph and Frank S. Carter. In the Lewes Fertilizer Company, Joseph was its first president and general manager. Carter became secretary and its last president. The involvement of Joseph and Carter in both the old Lewes

Fertilizer Company and the new Atlantic Fisheries Company suggests this may have been a reorganization of the company with a change in its operating plan, namely, a factory that processed fish bought from others who caught them.[101]

At the end of the 1938 season, a major change took place with the company to the west: Atlantic Fisheries was bought by J. Howard Smith, Inc., owned by brothers Gilbert and J. Howard Smith. Headquartered in Port Monmouth, New Jersey, it was one of the largest menhaden corporations on the Eastern seaboard. Although J. Howard's name was on the letterhead, Gilbert, the younger brother, ran the operations because he was more experienced with commercial fishing. Gilbert named the acquisition Fish Products Company and named his nephew and J. Howard's son, Otis Smith, its president. Possibly aware of the history of home-company versus foreign-company issue in Lewes, Otis Smith relocated and became a year-round resident of Lewes.[102]

Otis Smith would become a fixture in Lewes for the next thirty years. Born in Brooklyn, New York, in 1906, Smith graduated from New York Military Academy and attended Washington and Lee University followed by Brooklyn Law School. He immediately went to work for his family's company, first in Fernandina before moving to Lewes in early 1939. Ten years later, he was elected mayor of Lewes and reelected until 1968, when he declined reelection. A competitive and forceful leader in the menhaden industry, Smith was humble in his private life and did not publicize his accomplishments. He never said "no" to a worthy cause and became involved in many civic endeavors.[103]

The factory in Lewes was not the first venture of J. Howard Smith, Inc. into the menhaden industry in southern Delaware. During World War I, J. F. Bussells bought the Milford-based Diamond State Fish Products on the Mispillion River, fifteen miles from Lewes. With Bussells' death in July 1919 and the collapse in prices for fish products in 1920, the Milford plant went to a sheriff's auction. Two Lewes residents with a long history in its menhaden industry, William H. Bookhammer and John R. Baylis, purchased it and transferred the assets to a newly incorporated Diamond State Fish Products Company. Baylis soon relocated to Milford to be the general manager, while Bookhammer remained in Lewes as its president, which is why Diamond States Fish Products is sometimes considered a Lewes factory. The corporation acquired two steamers, which operated throughout the remainder of the decade, but the small operation was never financially sound. After the 1929 season, Diamond State Fish Products sold one of its ships—or half of its fleet—to J. Howard Smith, Inc. A small factory with only one fishing vessel, however, could not withstand the Great Depression, and J. Howard Smith, Inc. bought Diamond State Fish Products in 1931. Before the new owner could manage a single season, a storm destroyed the factory and forced abandonment. This first venture of the Smith family in Delaware was a failure but not a forecast of their future in Lewes.[104]

In 1954, a profitable year for the Lewes menhaden industry, Thomas and Richard Hayes were planning for Richard Hayes' son to soon take over Consolidated Fisheries. That autumn, the heir apparent was permanently disabled in a racing car accident that prevented him from ever managing the company. The dispirited and aging Hayes brothers sold their Consolidated Fisheries for $3.5 million to J. Howard Smith, Inc., the owners of Fish Products Company, the other factory on Lewes beach.* Otis Smith later recounted, "It was not for sale, and I did not seek the plant. Tom Hayes was just heartbroken and asked me if I would take it." With Smith's "extensive alterations" to his acquisition, the local newspaper correctly predicted that "an even larger amount of fish are expected to be landed in Lewes and processed at the two adjoining factories." Rather than merging Consolidated Fisheries into Fish Products, the Smiths established Seacoast Products Company with Otis Smith as president.[105]

From the 1920s to the 1960s, the Lewes menhaden companies' earnings ebbed and flowed with changes in both supply of menhaden in the ocean and the demand for fish oil and fish meal. The supply of menhaden products was subject to the whims of Mother Nature as is any commercial fishing operation. The profits also depended on the successes and failures of the consumers of menhaden products and their demand for them. Compounding the changes in supply was that oils from other sources could replace menhaden oil in a variety of uses, such as linseed oil in paints and petroleum lubricants in industry. Similarly, chemicals could and ultimately did replace fish meal in fertilizers in the 1930s. Poultry and swine feed did not need menhaden, especially considering that chicken and pigs do not eat fish naturally. Corn and other grains were easy alternatives.

---

*Soon after the sale, both Thomas and Richard Hayes died.

An example of this impact of decreasing demand was the 1920 season, which was a bust. Although it is true that not as many fish were landed as in some of the previous years, the real problem was the prices for menhaden products. Oil fell from $1.05 a gallon in 1919 to 40 cents, and fish scrap had a comparable decline. Such discouraging returns kept the Lewes factories closed for most of the 1921 season. Lewes Oil and Chemical Company, a locally owned firm, finally did open during the first week of September, but Hayes and Anderton's, a foreign plant, did not. For the following year, the Lewes factory remained open while the New York plant was shuttered. In1923, when the price of fish products rose and landings were the best in a decade.[106]

Despite steady prices for menhaden products, the 1924 season initially saw landings sputter. Fortunes changed in the beginning of August when the fishing, according to the *Milford Chronicle*, "is now rapidly improving and some good catches are being made." Such a spurt in menhaden landings gave rise to the newspaper's optimistic forecast, "[I]t now looks as if there will be plenty of fish from now on." Two weeks of good fishing does not a whole season make, however, and the Milford newspaper described it as "a very poor one, in fact, it is the poorest season they had in many years." Next year was similar, with poor fishing until the beginning of August, when the factories increased their output. With the recent past as a guide, the *Milford Chronicle* reported that the fishermen believed the "outlook for fishing this season looks very good." The fish that year were "fat" with oil, in part, because the previous season had been so slow. What kept the 1925 season from being one of the more successful ones, however, was the weather. High winds from September to November limited the steamers to only two or three days of good fishing a week. Still, the *Chronicle* reported that the fisheries thought "the past season had been fairly good, much better than last."[107]

The fair-to-good, if not great, fishing lasted for the next four seasons. This changed in 1931 to 1934. These four years were dismal because of the exceedingly poor market conditions for menhaden oil. The normal price of 38 cents to 40 cents per gallon had collapsed to 15 cents in the spring of 1931. The oil tanks were at capacity from the previous season. The fisheries initially decided to sell the oil at a deflated price and embark on another fishing season. In mid-season, Consolidated Fisheries and Atlantic Fisheries opted to shutter their factories and wait for an improvement in market prices, but the depressed prices continued. The weakening of the menhaden oil market was not a temporary phenomenon but part of the national economic conditions of the Depression. As industries throughout the country collapsed, the demand for fish oil for industrial use plummeted. Faced with operating at a loss, neither Consolidated Fisheries Company nor Atlantic Fisheries Company opened for the 1932 season. The Hayes brothers would never open the old factory they had bought in 1917 from Coast Fish Oil and Fertilizer Company and relied solely on the factory they acquired from Delaware Fish Oil Company. The owners of Consolidated Fisheries and Atlantic Fisheries appeared at the start of the season before the Lewes commissioners to request a reduction in rent. The request was tabled. They returned in August at the height of the "season" and asked that their rent be reduced by at least 40 percent, to which the town agreed. Resigned to a deflated market for fish oil, the plants reopened in 1933 and continued to operate without interruption until World War II. Each year was more successful than the previous one.[108]

Reflecting this improved profitability, Consolidated Fisheries Company built a new factory. At the end of the 1937 season, the unused Coast Fish Oil and Fertilizer Company building was destroyed by fire. The Hayes brothers had closed the plant in 1932 and relied only on the old Breakwater Fisheries factory. In place of the burnt remnants, the Hayes brothers built "the largest menhaden processing plant in the United States." According to the *Delaware Coast News*, "The latest and most modern equipment, including an enormous steel and glass enclosed factory covering a floor space of 10,500 square feet, and a 17,000-foot-long dock . . . have replaced the old wooden buildings known as the 'Coast Oil Company' which were erected in 1912." After this factory was fully operational in 1938, the Hayes brothers decommissioned and razed their other plant.[109]

The advent of World War II saw a resurgence of the menhaden industry generally and thus in Lewes specifically. As the national economy recovered from the Depression and as the mobilization efforts needed more menhaden products, the demand for them increased. The immediate postwar years saw a rapid growth of the Atlantic menhaden fishery. The impetus, however, occurred 3,000 miles away with the collapse of the pilchard fishery off the California coast. Like menhaden, pilchard are bony, oily fish that swim in large schools within forty to fifty miles offshore. Juvenile pilchard are "sardines" and thus are not exclusively factory fish. The pilchard fishery was insignificant prior to World War I but grew until the Fish and Wildlife Service would declare that the Pacific pilchard supported the country's largest fishery from 1933 through 1945. The run ended in 1946 when "the pilchard fishery experienced the worst season in its history." *Nature* magazine reported that "there was a disastrous failure of the fishery during the 1947-48 season, and . . . there seems at present [1953] little hope of a major recovery. . . ." Into this vacuum, in 1946, the menhaden catch was the largest ever. Two years later, the Atlantic menhaden had officially surpassed the pilchard as the nation's largest fishery and, in 1953, the menhaden fishery landed 1.7 *billion* pounds compared to only 9 *million* pounds of pilchard.[110]

A nation-wide growth of the menhaden fishery during the 1950s was mirrored in Lewes (see table 1).

Table 1. Menhaden Landings in Lewes

Year	Lewes Landing in Millions of Pounds
1945	170
1952	210
1953	360
1955	274
1956	404
1957	286
1960	281

The year 1953 marked a milestone for Lewes. A *Delaware Coast News* claimed, "LEWES IS RATED THE NO. ONE FISHING PORT IN THE WHOLE NATION." The ensuing story featured information from a Fish and Wildlife Service press release that reported the 360 million pounds landed in Lewes made it "the outstanding fishing port in 1953, in volume of landings." Lewes had overtaken San Pedro, California, which had been in first place for many years. The Associated Press ran the story nationally: "This ancient little Delaware town, home base to part of the fleet that searches for fish you never heard of, boasts proudly today the title No. 1 fishing port in the whole United States of America." The millions of pounds of menhaden put "Lewes ahead of such far-famed ports as San Pedro, San Diego, and San Francisco, Cal., Gloucester and Boston, Mass."[111]

Four years later, in 1957, a local newspaper heralded, "LEWES CAN CLAIM TITLE AS THE NATION'S NUMBER ONE FISHING PORT" with 404,489,200 pounds of fish. As with 1953, San Pedro landed the second-largest tonnage. In most other years in the 1950s, Lewes was second to San Pedro (see table 2).

Table 2: National Rank of Lewes in Menhaden Landings

Year	Lewes Landings in Millions of Pounds	National Rank
1945	170	#6
1952	210	#2
1953	360	#1
1955	274	#3
1956	404	#1
1957	286	#2
1960	281	#2

While edging out San Pedro for only two of six years in the 1950s Lewes still exaggerated its status and claimed to have been the number one fishing port in the entire country.[112]

This success in the 1950s occurred after years of corporate struggles and changes, of fluctuating markets for menhaden products and, of course, from unpredictable numbers of menhaden in the ocean.

CHAPTER 10

Something Fishy in Politics

Beginning with the favorable lease for the first home company in 1911 and lasting until the late 1930s, the Lewes menhaden industry enjoyed the support of the local political leaders. The commissioners leased bayfront land to the companies, whose annual rents grew the town's treasury. Moreover, elected officials actively participated in the operation of the various home companies. James T. Thompson, former president and general manager of the Delaware Fish Oil Company for over a decade, was elected to twenty-nine one-year terms as mayor. His last election was in January 1930, only five months before he died. The town selected Ulysses W. Hocker to replace him; despite no direct involvement with the fish factories, the new mayor was generally supportive of them. With declining town revenues because of the Great Depression, 40 percent of Hocker's budget came from the menhaden companies in rent and utility payments. Reflective of the Thompson years, Hocker faced no opposition in subsequent elections. The tranquility of the Hocker years, however, was upset when fish factories entered town politics.[113]

When Hocker decided not to seek reelection in January 1936, Lewes's era of elections without opposition ended. Without Hocker in the race, the *Delaware Coast News* claimed it was "thought by all citizens to be a walk-over" for William E. Walsh. Born in 1878, Walsh had little formal education, leaving his county school after the third grade. But he was a born entrepreneur, marketing innovative products and services. At the turn of the century, his retail bicycle shop began selling Buicks, Chevrolets, and Cadillacs. Walsh started the first motion picture theaters in Lewes, Georgetown, and Milton. From a furniture store he co-owned, Walsh sold major electrical appliances. Walsh's current project was to acquire leases directly east from the town of Lewes to build beachfront cottages for second homeowners. His longest lasting contribution to the fabric of Lewes was the residential development that became known as "Lewes Beach Cottage Colony." When the 1936 election approached, Walsh had been serving on the town commission for fourteen years.[114]

Where Menhaden Was King

Walsh's opponent, David W. Burbage, was twelve years older and a maritime legend in Lewes. Raised on the Lewes bayfront in a house near the Iron Pier, he, at the youthful age of twenty-one, started up D. W. Burbage & Co., a firm that provided services and supplies to vessels stopping in Lewes on their way to and from Philadelphia. Originally using rowboats to ferry materials and information to ships at anchor in Lewes harbor, the company graduated to motorboats. His office was located above the local Western Union branch, making it easy for him to communicate with ship owners, brokers, shippers, consignees, and bankers. He was one of the principals behind the incorporation of the Lewes Fisheries Company and first president of the Coast Fish Oil and Fertilizer Company. Although Burbage had retired and sold his company in 1928, the governor appointed him the harbor master in 1935.[115]

The Lewes government consisted of a mayor and four commissioners, all serving two-year terms. The mayor was elected every two years, and a set of two commissioners faced the voters every year. The elections were held annually on the first Saturday in January, even if that Saturday happened to fall on New Year's Day. To be eligible to vote in municipal elections, an adult needed to pay an annual "capitation" tax or "head" tax. This was one of the major revenue streams for the town as every adult in 1936 had to pay $4. Essentially it was a flat tax on each person living in Lewes and theoretically served to collect some money from people who did not have taxable items, such as a renter who owned no type of real property.

Two months before the 1936 election, storms over the leases to the menhaden companies began to churn the political waters. Consolidated Fisheries Company had two leases for bayfront land, one acquired from the Coast Fish Oil and Fertilizer Company, the other from Breakwater Fisheries Company. Both agreements were set to expire but contained renewal options, The Coast Fish Oil and Fertilizer Company lease was renewed without delay or complication. Executing the renewal option for the Breakwater Fisheries lease, however, was not going to be so routine.[116]

Candidate Burbage, because of his earlier involvement with menhaden companies, was thought to support renewing the Breakwater Fisheries lease--but he never stated a position. In contrast, Walsh, who had no maritime experience, was assumed to be opposed to renewing the second lease because his current business venture in constructing beachfront homes depended on people's desire to buy, and the odors emanating from the menhaden plants lessened that desire. Like his opponent, Walsh never publicized his position. After the campaign hoopla, Burbage upset the favored Walsh by a narrow 16-vote margin, 283-267. In a front-page article, the *Delaware Coast News* claimed, "It is well known at the present time that the Hayes Brothers [owners of Consolidated Fisheries Company] had much to do with the election." It went on to imply that they had paid the $4 in past due capitation taxes for between 150 and 200 African American voters and for another fifteen bootleggers: "It is our opinion that the Hayes Brothers could conveniently pay out less than $1000 . . . to buy votes" and sway the election. Walsh himself believed that his perceived opposition to the renewal of the lease had caused his narrow loss of the mayoral election.[117]

As expected, the town under the new mayor quickly approved the renewal of the old Breakwater Fisheries lease for another twenty years. Later that year, the Hayes Brothers negotiated a lease that combined its existing leases into one. The lease would extend thirty-five years to 1971, allowing Consolidated Fisheries the right of renewal for another thirty years or until 2001. There were the same expiration terms as the one under which Lewes' other fish plant, Atlantic Fisheries, was operating, and thus the agreements for both fish plants would expire simultaneously in 2001.[118]

Theodore Bryan and Harvey Baker were elected commissioners in 1936. Since Bryan reportedly sold over $500 of ice to fisheries each year, he was considered an ally of Burbage and supporter of the menhaden industry. Baker, on the other hand, was considered independent. The two holdovers on the commission supported Walsh in the election and formed an opposition bloc to Burbage. The *Delaware Coast News* reported that the commission had "been unable to accomplish anything due to the fact that the Commissioners were split in two ways." This soon changed. After nearly three months in office, Baker resigned from the commission to become the supervisor of streets in Lewes. Edward Suthard replaced Baker, and the *Delaware Coast News'* headline on the front page read, "MAYOR BURBAGE NOW CONTROLS THE LEWES TOWN COUNCIL." It appeared that the commission would continue its support of the menhaden industry, at least for another six years.[119]

During Burbage's tenure as mayor, town politics was filled with bitterness, and the animosity between factions became more intense.

During this period of political turmoil, William E. Walsh, who Burbage had defeated, became mayor in January 1938. In November, Joseph Jett of the Menhaden Company of Reedville, Virginia, requested a lease to build a plant, which would bring the total in Lewes to three and thus reintroduce an old point of contention. The proposed lease would cover the land between the U. S. Coast Guard Station and Atlantic Fisheries that J. Howard Smith, Inc. had just purchased. Jett and his family owned and operated several fishing steamers and had been bringing their catches to the Atlantic Fisheries. Due to the sale of the company to the Smith family, who owned and operated their own boats, the Jetts needed an alternative processing site and wanted a factory for their fish.

During a commission meeting, Jett explained that the new factory would be a modern facility costing about $100,000. This factory would employ the latest technology to eliminate *"most* of the odor" [emphasis added], and Jett promised that all Army Corps of Engineers' water regulations laws would be strictly adhered to. The lease itself would bind his company to these standards. According to the *Delaware Pilot*, the commissioners believed that the public overwhelmingly supported the third factory, provided its lease ran concurrently with the lease of the existing plants, since there was no legal way to remove the factories already on the bayfront. Believing two other lease holders might sublet to the Menhaden Company, a commissioner argued that it was not "whether or not another fish plant was desirable" but "whether or not the municipality wanted the factory with or without the revenues." A local newspaper acknowledged the latent effort to promote tourism: "The development of the beachfront within the curve of Cape Henlopen, which is now occupied by the fish factories, as a resort colony of hotels and cottages, is definitely much to be desired." Since the two current factories already had long-term leases that expired simultaneously in 2001, "there seemed nothing to do to realize the resort project until after this generation is gone. It is hoped that in some distant day after the expiration of the sixty-three years when the present leases run out, that future Lewes residents may enjoy the benefits to be procured from a cottage colony."[120]

News of the proposal for the third factory quickly spread through Lewes and irate citizens canvassed the town to drum up opposition. Leading the protest was Paul F. Carpenter, a native Lewestowner who was elected president of the local chamber of commerce in 1937, a year after it reopened, and who had previously headed the organization before it folded due to the Depression. Carpenter's Ford dealership in Lewes also closed and, after running a poultry plant, he became a supervisor in the state highway department. In total, he was president of the chamber more than fifteen years, and he used that platform to encourage vacationers to the town, especially through his persistent advocacy of ferry service between Lewes and Cape May.[121]

To protest the third factory, Carpenter called a meeting for the public to voice an opinion. A mere five days after Jett's request for the additional factory, November 22, a crowd of ninety-two people converged on the fire hall. Of those attending, only fifty-two signed a petition against the new factory. A majority demanded a town referendum. The complaints focused on three problems with the fish plants. The most obvious was the pollution of the "air and waterways" of Lewes, while another was the "class of out-of-state Negro labor employed by the fish factories." The third point reflected the home vs. foreign factories wars twenty-years earlier when one participant sarcastically asked, "Why is it the fish houses didn't stink when Lewestowners owned them?" One attendee heatedly demanded to know why the commission would make such a decision so critical to the residents and property owners of Lewes without input from the citizens. Two members of the commission attended the rally, Mayor Walsh and Commissioner J. Orton Marshall. The latter called the meeting's support of a referendum "unfair" since only "objectors" were at the fire hall that night.

The mayor did not defend the lease outright nor did he address any of the long-standing criticisms, preferring to wait until the chamber of commerce conducted a door-to-door canvass. He added, however, that waiting may not be an option since the Pennsylvania Railroad reportedly had offered to sublet to Jett's Menhaden Company some of its bayfront land. Most importantly, the Jetts were willing to pay $1,200 annually in rent, more than the other plants were paying. The figure would jump to a total of $5,000 when the purchase of city electricity and water were considered. This would be 15 percent of the town's total revenue.[122]

Following this meeting, the chamber of commerce flooded the town with a broadside spurring the citizens to fight against the third factory. The handbill argued that the current fish factories offered no benefits to Lewes. They have "polluted the air we breath [sic] . . . and our waterways . . . [and] inflicted a pestilence of fish house flies upon us." Seining the menhaden "destroyed our food fish." These fish oil plants are "the cause of a serious threat to the public order and decency of our town through the low class of employees which they have brought into our midst from outside points." Because of this environment, visitors "have been driven away by the factories." The chamber erroneously claimed that both the mayor and Commissioner Marshall had supported the factory during the meeting, and that the two politicians intended to inflict another factory on Lewes beach "despite your decision to the contrary." A second flyer was addressed to the "Citizens of Lewes" and asked "It is up to you. What are you going to do about it?" The leaflet included an invective against the Board of Commissioners who "regard the public affairs as solely their business and take the attitude that these matters are none of your business." The circular concluded that the citizens needed to decide whether "your comfort, your future welfare, and the future prosperity of our hometown shall be further seriously damaged by the erection of a new public nuisance, a new fish factory." These leaflets were part of the chamber's canvass to gather as many signatures as possible on a protest petition.[123]

The local controversy soon escalated into a statewide issue. A major Wilmington newspaper weighed in against the new factory, its editorial claiming that "Lewes must decide whether the town is to continue as a delightful summer resort." While sympathetic to new industries, it continued that such support should "exclude those with noisome features that will retard the residential development of the town as well as those along the strand during the vacation months." Despite the best efforts of the factories, "they have been unable to check the outpouring of fumes that are very close to nauseating. This stench is wafted as far away as Rehoboth Beach. . . ." Reflecting this sentiment, Mary Wilson Thompson, a prominent Wilmington socialite who owned a second home in Rehoboth Beach, sent a letter in support of the chamber's effort. She said that the odor forced her to close the windows of her pre-air-conditioned house. With a variety of statewide civic and political involvements, Thompson wrote that she "recently [had] urged an injunction against the reopening of the [current] fish factories as a public nuisance." In sum, she wanted "the citizens of Lewes to hold fast and to absolutely refuse the adding of a third plant at this place." With her statewide contacts, she was probably the main reason why the otherwise local issue rapidly blossomed statewide with Wilmington newspapers reporting on the controversy and editorializing against the third factory.[124]

Ten days after the first protest meeting, Carpenter chaired a second one. Although the results of a door-to-door canvass were promised, the project had not yet been completed. Mayor Walsh again attended. He had claimed earlier that he was neutral in the controversy, but some had read this "neutrality" as tacit support for the additional factory. He had indeed spoken of the revenue a third factory would bring to the depleted town coffers. These people felt betrayed since he had been viewed as opposing the renewal of the Consolidated Fisheries lease earlier in the decade. A letter to Walsh asked, "If you, Mr. Mayor, opposed and fought the lease of the old company some two or three years ago, and suffered a temporary defeat to your ambition to be mayor of Lewes, why do you favor this new nuisance?" Another asked more bluntly, "Tell us, Mr. Mayor, why this sudden change of heart?" At the meeting, disavowing his supposed neutrality, Walsh shocked some when he announced that he was opposed to the third factory. He said that he always opposed a third factory but had indeed wondered about the impact of the revenue to the town. Now, he had concluded that rent from beachfront cottages would offset any revenue from a third factory. The mayor also stated that he did "not believe that any fish factory can be made completely odorless . . . I am opposed to granting any additional person or persons a lease for erecting another fish factory." Applause from the receptive audience greeted his remarks, and several people who had criticized the mayor for his failure to oppose the factory apologized.[125]

The Lewes board of commissioners convened three days later. One of the first items on the agenda was for Carpenter to present his petition against the third factory with 281 signatures. To allow time to complete the canvass, which he believed would show that most of the town opposed a third factory, the chamber president asked that a commission vote on the lease be tabled for two weeks. Commissioner Thomas Virden moved to grant Carpenter the additional time. On a roll call vote, the motion failed two to three. Voting "yea" were commissioner Theodore R. Bryan and Mayor Walsh; voting "nay" were commissioners Virden, Frank S. Carter, and J. Orton Marshall. When Marshall voted against additional time, Carpenter heatedly accused the commissioner of going back on his word and creating a "situation of near riot proportions." When order returned, a motion to hold a referendum on the lease at the municipal election also was defeated. The meeting then considered the request for a lease from Jetts' Menhaden Company in Virginia, at twice the per foot price being paid by the other two companies. The resolution to accept the proposal contained this justification: "It is desirable to increase the revenue to the Town of Lewes wherever possible without expense to the taxpayers." Commissioner Virden dismissed the petitions from the chamber of commerce because they lacked the signatures of most taxpayers. When the final vote was taken, Mayor Walsh voted "nay" against the four commissioners voting "yea." The controversial lease was formally and finally approved.[126]

CHAPTER 11

The People Speak

The town commission's approval of the lease for a third factory did not end the controversy and may in fact have been the key to David Burbage's upset victory in the 1936 mayoral election. The ongoing debate over the third factory had awakened a sleeping giant, and it would not go back to bed, especially since another election for two commissioners was less than a month away, potentially deciding the future of the menhaden industry in Lewes.

Indicative of the emotional intensity over the factories, ideas about the possibility of injunctions or impeachment were flying around. Mayor Walsh announced that he had vigorously opposed the new lease and vowed not to sign it. Some townspeople pointed out that the location for the lease was the revered burial site of sailors from an almost forgotten period: "Can the town ruthlessly permit the building of a fish plant over the bodies of hundreds of sailors buried on our shores?" Pragmatically, some hoped that the "dearly bought revenue" would permit the reduction of the capitation tax. Two lessees, Thomas H. Jett Jr. and Joseph C. Jett Jr., vice president and secretary respectively of the Menhaden Company, had come to Lewes to await, and possibly influence, the decision. They pledged, "We will comply with the commissioners' demand for 'an odorless and sanitary plant' so far as possible but no fish plant has ever been built without some odor." Unimpressed, Paul Carpenter, the chamber president opposing the plan, said, "We will do everything possible to have the wishes of our people upheld." His vehicle for these wishes would be the municipal elections on January 7 when two incumbent commissioners who supported the lease, Frank S. Carter and J. Orton Marshall, would be up for reelection.[127]

To explain their decision, the four commissioners issued a detailed statement on the fish factories. For Carter and Marshall, the statement would help them defend their votes during the looming campaign. The original leases to all three fisheries dating back to the 1910s would expire in 2001 without the possibility of automatic renewal. The commissioners argued that the issues surrounding the fisheries could be rectified. "There is no doubt in our minds that the objectionable features to a fish factory operated along modern lines can be curtailed, eliminating practically all nauseating odors and water pollution." The commissioners also identified three or four more pieces of leased land that could be sublet to the Jetts, although any sublease would not produce additional revenue for Lewes. Countering Walsh's argument that revenue from cottages would offset the lost revenue of a third factory, the commissioners divided the bayfront into a residential beach with cottages and an industrial beach with fish factories. Of the two beaches, the industrial beach would bring in far more revenue than the residential beach, $4,800 to $2,600 annually. The third factory would add $1,000 to the industrial beach funds, bringing the total to $5,800 per year. The commissioners also recognized that some viewed the fish factories on the industrial beach as a curse, "which unfortunate though it must be endured for sixty-three (63) more years."[128]

This did not satisfy opponents to the third factory. Carpenter analyzed each paragraph of the lease and concluded that "the terms . . . break every promise made by the Commissioners and are an insult to the intelligence of our citizenry." He pointed out that the lease itself called for a yearly rental of $842. Not only was this less than the commissioners had promised, it also was about half of Consolidated Fisheries Company's rent. Carpenter sarcastically remarked that Lewes would "get the odor at half price." Another paragraph stipulated that the Jetts would build a "first-class plant equipped in a modern manner . . . and . . . nearly odorless as is reasonably practical." Finding out what this phrase meant, in Carpenter's view, is as "difficult as finding an answer to the question, "How high is up?"' When a provision called for purification and disposal of wastewater to meet Army Corps of Engineers requirements, Carpenter pointed out that those regulations are only concerned about the waters of Delaware Bay and thus would permit construction of a "rancid dump hole" onshore for putrefying waste. While the commissioners could authorize an inspection of the factories "at any time," the inspectors could only call attention to problems; any correction would be at the discretion of the Jetts.

The last section was, Carpenter concluded, "the most fantastic and absurd clause (Paragraph Fifteen) of the lease. It is readily understood why this paragraph would be last as it winds up as a most ridiculous attempt to draw a lease." Realizing that the other fish factories might indeed leave Lewes before the end of their leases, the commissioners wanted a clause to buy the Menhaden Company out of the remainder of its agreement. If the Jetts' plant ever became the only remaining fish factory, the town could, upon a twelve-month notice, terminate the lease. In exchange, Lewes would reimburse the Menhaden Company for the actual cost of the factory and any improvements or repairs plus 3 percent annual interest from the date of each expenditure. Carpenter computed what this meant if the town bought back the lease after a hypothetical thirty-three years: the city would have received $27,786 in rent but was obligated to pay $475,000 for the cost of the plants and any improvements or repairs. He reiterated, "Just try to comprehend those figures—$475,000.00 plus 3 percent interest against $27,786.00" Almost as a side note, but still twisting the knife, he added, "The lease fails to provide whether or not the interest shall be compounded." Carpenter said that he had had trouble obtaining a copy of the lease and labelled the delay an "attempt of Commissioner Marshall to conceal it . . . [and this analysis of it] reveals why the lease should be concealed as far as the Commissioners are concerned." The anger over the third factory now focused on Paragraph Fifteen. Flyers, sometimes using violent terms, flooded the town protesting the offending section.[129]

When the *Delaware Coast News* published Carpenter's examination of the lease, it did so with a banner headline stretching from edge to edge of the front page: "Rental of New Fish Factory Surprise to Citizens." On December 23, Carpenter announced that legal notice had been served on the Menhaden Company. He said they were "filing a bill in equity enjoining your company from erecting a fish factory." He ominously warned, "If you proceed to erect a factory you will do so at your own peril." The exact legal basis of the complaint is murky, other than the infamous Paragraph Fifteen could be disproportionately punitive to the town. Yet he was confident of success because, he said, "We have the backing of the best people of our town as well as in other parts of the state, people who are genuinely interested in the development of our 308-year-old town, more than we can say of our own town commissioners." He also announced a third citizens' meeting for the following week to nominate candidates who will oppose the two commissioners whose terms were expiring, Carter and Marshall.[130]

As a result of the controversy about Paragraph Fifteen, the four commissioners convened a special meeting at 11:00 a.m. on Christmas

Where Menhaden Was King

Eve and quickly voted to delete and nullify it. The resolution stated that the Menhaden Company had asked for it to be removed. An unsigned flyer explained the situation: "Commissioner 'Edgar Bergen' Carter pulled all strings and pushed 3 valves down and 'Charlie McCarthy' Marshall, along with Self-Opinionated Virden and 'Yes Man' Bryan responded by voting to strike entirely Clause 15 of 3rd Fish House Lease."* The removal of this clause did not mollify protesters because "the stricken clause removes any likelihood of the town ever getting rid of the new plant before the next century."[131]

The question of a third menhaden factory on the bayfront was the dominant issue in the 1939 election of two commissioners. Carter and Marshall filed for reelection as supporters of the factory. In opposition, two new candidates running together as a slate were Edward J. Suthard and Marshall Hazzard. Suthard had previously served as commissioner when he was appointed to fill the unexpired term that secured Mayor Burbage his majority to renew the Consolidated Fish Company leases. Hazzard was a life-long resident of Lewes and had represented the area in the state legislature. Beyond a general reform platform, the Suthard-Hazzard slate supported the menhaden industry but opposed an additional factory. While not Lewes residents, the Hayes brothers, owners of Consolidated Fisheries, did not hide their strong support of Suthard and Hazzard. One of their leaflets asserted, "It is a well known fact these factories should be kept here and not removed. Though to an extent they do pollute our air and water. Should a few silly bathers have to be the cause of their removal? Emphatically, NO!" Their campaign flyer also praised Richard and Thomas Hayes as being well known to the community and as being good employers paying good wages.[132]

Keeping the current factories while opposing a new one was a solution that did not satisfy those Lewestowners who wanted to rid the town of all factories and their foul air and polluted bay waters. On December 29, Carpenter convened yet another opposition meeting in the firehouse to select candidates for the two open commissioner positions. In response to Carpenter's request for possible nominations, those attending the meeting suggested six names: Charles D. Beebe, Paul C. Carpenter, Nathaniel H. Evans, Charles V. Jones, Daniel D. J. Littleton, and Irvin Maull. On the ballot for nominees, the newly formed Citizens

---

*Edgar Bergen was a famous ventriloquist in the 1930s whose puppet was Charlie McCarthy.

Committee also added the names of the four candidates who had already filed: Frank S. Carter, Marshall Hazzard, J. Orton Marshall, and Edward J. Suthard. By secret ballot, voters could select two nominees. Jones came out on top, with twenty-six votes, Beebe in second place with eighteen. Suthard was third with twelve votes. Sharing the slate with Suthard, who wanted to keep the two current factories, was Hazzard, with eleven votes. Interestingly, Carpenter, who had called the meeting as the acknowledged leader of the opposition to the factories, received only three votes. Two votes were cast for incumbent commissioners who supported the additional factory. Maybe indicative of the regard for him, Orton Marshall was the only one on the ballot who did not receive a single vote. Instead, the name of another incumbent commissioner was a write-in. Despite a strong minority wanting to retain the two current factories, the assembly went on record as being opposed to all fish factories, not just the third new one. To support the protest financially, ten people in attendance pledged donations to the "Fighting Fund."[133]

The pre-election maneuvering produced three slates, each with a different approach to the fish factories: 1) add a third factory (Carter and Marshall); 2) oppose a new factory but keep the current two (Suthard and Hazzard); and 3) oppose all factories (Beebe and Jones). Anonymous and signed flyers flooded the town promoting or attacking one slate or the other. The handbills were primarily aimed against Carter and Marshall, accusing them of various forms of corruption and otherwise impugning their honesty and integrity, while resurrecting the board's recent increase of the head tax to $5 or the highest in the country. A letter to the *Delaware Pilot* claimed that one flyer was "more distasteful to decent persons than the smell of a dozen fish factories." For Suthard and Marshall, it was alleged that the Hayes brothers had committed as much as $10,000 to the ticket's campaign, some of which would be used to sway the African American votes. The Beebe-Jones ticket countered:

> We believe that you [African American voters] should be treated as human beings and not something to be bought on election day. Also, we believe that you should have a special [police] officer in your locality during the summer months and that that officer should be one of your own selection. It might be well to add that if we had no fish factories you would need no special officer.

The vitriol between the three slates was so intense that the town requested the state police to oversee the election. And the *Delaware Pilot* did report that "two state policemen were on hand to see that no riots occurred."[134]

When the results were tallied on Saturday afternoon, January 7, 1939, in what a Wilmington newspaper called "the stormiest election in the history of the town," Carter (277 votes) and Marshall (272 votes) were re-elected. Because they won with a sizable number of combined votes, Carter and Marshall claimed that the people approved a third factory. Opponents disagreed, arguing that the two slates opposing the third factory (Jones-Beebe and Suthard-Hazzard) when combined received more votes (561) than Carter-Marshall (549) and concluding that "a slight majority of those who participated in the election opposed a new fish plant." The Jones-Beebe team opposed to all factories came in last place with a combined total of 230 votes. A post-election analysis in a Wilmington newspaper suggested that the $5 head tax had kept many people from voting, and thus the vote did not reflect the true sentiments of the town. Some claimed that the incumbents were elected only through "bought votes." Others maintained that the voters were "confused" by the two platforms opposing the third factory. Denying that the third factory was a *fait accompli* despite the vote, the chamber of commerce under Carpenter outlined three months later its agenda for the coming years and included "continued efforts toward the elimination of fish houses at Lewes and any other objectionable industry barring the ultimate development of the Delaware Capes' [sic] resort."[135]

It was an overwhelming landslide; more than a two-to-one majority had endorsed menhaden plants on the Lewes bayfront and by implication was willing to accept the negative consequences of obnoxious odors, polluted waters, and possibly a higher level of crime. The citizens had spoken, and they voted that the menhaden industry, with its benefits to the Lewes economy, was more important than ridding their community of polluted air and water.

CHAPTER 12

The Fight Continues

Losing the battle of the 1939 election did not mean losing the war to stop the third factory, and opponents continued to seek ways to block it. Since the Army Corps of Engineers needed to approve any construction in navigable rivers and bay, the Menhaden Company applied for a permit from the agency to construct a pier into the Delaware Bay between the piers of the U. S. Coast Guard to the west and of the Fish Products Company to the east. The agency, adhering to its normal procedures, issued a public notice of the application to construct a pier, and asked for comments by the first week in January. As emotions from the electioneering cooled, the opponents turned their energies to a way to impede the third factory–opposition to its pier.[136]

Within the ten-day response window, the Corps of Engineers received several written objections to the construction of the pier. John W. Marshall, who was captain of a party boat that took sportsmen out for deep-sea fishing, objected to the 1200-foot pier and a rumored 40-foot-high elevator at the end of it. He argued that this building and any fishing steamers docked along the side of the pier would obstruct the view of the of the bay from the U. S. Coast Guard's 35-foot lookout tower. A petition signed by twelve other party boat operators endorsed Marshall's reasoning, adding that the plans should not be approved because the exact dimensions of the elevator were not included.[137]

Because of strong tides and high winds, menhaden vessels frequently had to wait before docking. According to Irvin S. Maull, another party boat captain, this could delay launching Coast Guard boats, "perhaps causing unnecessary loss of life and property." Another petition with fifty-five signatures protested the pier mainly because of anticipated water pollution, although it acknowledged, without explanation, that the current fish factory piers also "constitute menace to navigation." One rumored argument was that the proposed pier would extend several hundred feet beyond any other pier in the area "bringing it very close, if not into, the main channel." Paul Carpenter, quickly and on the last day of the comment period, dashed off a one-sentence letter stating the chamber of commerce opposed the pier "as it would be a menace to navigation."[138]

To the east of the proposed pier was Fish Products Company of J. Howard Smith, Inc., whose owner, Gilbert Smith, wrote another letter to the Corps objecting to the proposed pier since it would not be in the center of the parcel but closer to the Smith's property than to the Coast Guard station. Smith wanted the Jetts to put the pier in the middle of their property, because he wanted to build another factory with a pier centered on the Smith bayfront. Without fully explaining what this new factory would produce, his letter stated that it would not be a menhaden fish oil factory but tantalized it as being "a very great help to the people of Lewes, as it will employ a great deal of labor in comparison with the Menhaden fish factories." As a result of this and the other written objections, Major C. W. Burlin of the Corps of Engineers issued notice of a hearing on the Menhaden Company's proposal at the Lewes firehouse.[139]

On a cold and blustery February morning, Burlin and three others from the Corps of Engineers welcomed forty-four people to the hearing on the proposed pier. The major stressed that the sole purpose was to hear objections that concerned navigation. Nuisance and other reasons for opposing the pier or its factory were not within the scope of the Corps of Engineers' responsibilities. U.S. Coast Guard Commander Frank E. Allison worried about his boats having only 278 feet to clear the proposed pier. The commander explained that a northwest wind and an easterly tide could carry a boat with momentum coming out of the Coast Guard's launch into the proposed dock. He estimated a 400-foot clearance was needed to safely maneuver a boat under those conditions. Burlin questioned Allison whether the proposed elevator for lifting the fish from the steamer "would obstruct your view to the east?" Allison answered, "Not very serious." He added, "I have already recommended better lookout facilities for that Station." This testimony undermined one of the major arguments of the opponents. Allison ended, "Evidence of the objectionable feature of the factory is not admissible, so I think that completes my statement." For Allison, "[T]he objectionable feature . . . no matter how much effort is made to reduce the smell and chemical gases [would exist] to cause annoyance to . . . [the seventeen Guard members and their families] that are living in the vicinity." Obnoxious fumes and odors, in other words, do not impede navigation.[140]

For the town of Lewes, Commissioner Virden testified, "There would be no objection by the commissioners of Lewes.... That represents the official opinion of the commissioners of Lewes." At Burlin's invitation, Paul Carpenter presented the chamber of commerce's opposition to the pier. In the event of a thunderstorm or a northwest wind, he explained, the Coast Guard must hurry out and face the possibility that their gasoline engines could stall because of the narrow space for maneuvering. He concluded by reiterating that the pier would hinder party boats sailing in and out to open sea. Disagreeing with Carpenter, a representative of the Lewes Anglers Association volunteered that the pier would not hamper the sport fishing boats getting in and out but that it could interfere with the Coast Guard boats. When Major Burlin questioned whether he had spoken with anyone from the Coast Guard station, the Anglers Association spokesman (a party boat captain), admitted that he had not and that it was his own opinion.[141]

When Burlin asked if anyone else wanted to speak, Gilbert P. Smith elaborated on his company's cryptic letter. He stated that the proposed pier would be 100 feet from his property and that the Fish Products Company had already applied for a permit to construct a pier in the middle of its own property. The Smith pier would not be for another menhaden factory, however: "It is a business which we talked over carefully at one of our meetings, and which we had in mind probably in a year or two, in erecting a pier and canning plant on the remaining 500 feet." Such a project would "mean a great deal to Lewes, for it is a good fish canning plant and will employ many good hands, and is somewhat a higher type of labor." A local newspaper estimated the factory would employ 300 laborers. Smith, however, declined to disclose what type of fish would be canned. The *Delaware Coast News* claimed the announcement of the new canning plant strengthened opponents to all fish factories because the new enterprise would "entail no water pollution or odor, nor otherwise objectionable features of fish plants." For navigation purposes, Smith's argument made little sense since it would mean moving the Jetts' pier over 100 feet closer to the Coast Guard station and would exacerbate any possible interference with the Guard's operations.[142]

About two months after the hearing, the Corps of Engineers granted the permit for the Jetts' pier providing that the length be reduced by 150 feet, apparently to mitigate interference with Coast Guard operations.

Also, the Menhaden Company had to complete its pier by the expiration of the permit, December 1942. When the Menhaden Company received permission for its pier, Joseph H. Jett said that construction would not begin for some time.[143]

As the expiration date approached, the Jetts requested an extension, acknowledging that the proposed factory had "encountered considerable opposition" from the people of Lewes. After the hearings, "the opposition continued for a long period of time but finally, as a result of the concessions made by Menhaden Company, the local opposition was minimized."* Additional delays came as World War II thwarted the effort to build a pier when the company could not obtain the needed materials and labor. Since the holdup in erecting the pier was no fault of the Menhaden Company, the extension was warranted. This time the public notice attracted no opposition, and the Corps of Engineers extended the permit for another three years.[144]

Even with this additional time, though, the Menhaden Company did not build the pier nor did it ever build a fish factory on the land it had leased from Lewes. The reasons remain obscure.* It was not because of renewed opposition from the Lewestowners. The attorney who represented the company, Howard M. Long, a Philadelphia lawyer with a home on Lewes Beach, was once a leading opponent to a third fish plant. In 1938, just eight days after the Jetts had asked for a lease from the town, a letter from Long appeared in the *Delaware Coast News*. After outlining the pleasant and attractive aspects of Lewes, Long wrote about the negative impact of "the menhaden factories, which pollute both the air and the waterways–only one sort of fly in the ointment, and that the fish-house fly." When the announcement of a meeting to

---

*Whatever concessions the Menhaden Company made to "minimize" local opposition were not uncovered during this author's research. Nor was the motivation for the fish company to make concessions.

*In 1953, an attorney wrote the Town of Lewes on behalf of the Jett family: "I have heard that this land was designated as a memorial burying ground for unknown soldiers subsequent to the granting of the lease to the Menhaden Company, ... [and] the real purpose of our employment was to determine about the burying ground." In sum, he wanted to know "if the lease is at present honored by the Town." [Robert W. Tunnell to Otis H. Smith, November 18, 1953, "Legal Correspondence, 1947-1954," Management and Operation of Smith Companies, 1946-1954, Otis Smith Papers, Lewes Historical Society, Lewes, Delaware.] The Jetts continued to pay the $842 annual rent for the duration of the war and retained Lewes' permission to build a third factory into the post-war years. The final legal nail was driven into the third-factory coffin in 1963. On October 27, the Menhaden company wrote to the commissioners that it was exercising its option of section 14 to terminate the lease with sixty days written notice. The Menhaden Company terminated and surrendered the property on December 31, 1960. [Menhaden Company to Board of Commissioners of Lewes, October 27, 1960, "M," Subject Files of the Mayor of Lewes,1957-1969, Otis Smith Papers.]

oppose the Jett plant was announced, the *Delaware Coast News* front-page headline blared, "HOWARD M. LONG, ESQ., SPEAKER AT CITIZEN'S MEETING TO BE HELD IN AUDITORIUM." Yet three years later, this highly visible and vocal opponent of the Jetts had become their legal advocate before the Corps of Engineers.[145]

After failing to stop the third menhaden factory through the Corps of Engineers, the opponents found a new reason for their cause: the factory would be on hallowed ground. Paul Carpenter pointed out that the plant would be located on the burial grounds of sailors and seamen. The graveyard had briefly surfaced as an issue when the lease controversy was just beginning to heat up in 1939. Buried on the inside pages of the *Delaware Coast News* of the December 9 edition was a small article listing various reasons for objection to the third lease. Older residents remembered the proposed factory site as a revered burial ground for sailors of an almost forgotten era. Other residents remembered "yawning, bone-filled graves." And some were asking, "Can the town ruthlessly permit the building of a fish plant over the grave of dead sailors buried on our shores?" During the ensuing months of hot debate over the election and about the pier, the issue of the sailors' cemetery lay mainly dormant.[146]

The cemetery was created before World War I, when a body washed up on the shore and was buried above the high-water mark close to where it was found. This gave way to the establishment of a formal burial ground for American seamen from the days of sailing ships. It reportedly also included scores of immigrants who died in the Quarantine Station and of seamen who died in an old government hospital at the Iron Pier. The graveyard was spread along 200 feet of fenced bayfront with wooden grave markers, painted white with black letters. By the end of World War I, all surface signs on the burial site had disappeared. Reportedly at least four or five hundred bodies were buried there, with some estimates as high as eight hundred. The existence and location of the burial ground revived the controversy over a third factory.

Carpenter enlisted the aid of U. S. Senator John G. Townsend to explore whether Lewes could legally lease for commercial purposes land that had been designated a cemetery. When it was determined that no federal or state law prohibited this, Townsend's colleague, U. S. Senator James H. Hughes, upped the ante and warned, "But there is remedy in law." With this background, a movement began in Delaware to erect a monument to the "Unknown Sailor" on the cemetery site.[147]

One of the two existing fish plants, probably Consolidated Fisheries and its owner Thomas Hayes, lobbied the General Assembly in Dover to bring about the sailors' monument, eliminating any additional competition in Lewes. Within a month, Senate Bill 320 raced through the house and senate. So rushed was the process that the commissioners of Lewes learned of it from Hayes only *after* both houses had passed the bill. Governor Richard C. McMullen signed it in May 1939, setting aside a tract of public lands "as a memorial cemetery for the burial of sailors and shall be maintained *solely* [emphasis added] for that purpose. The cemetery shall be known as the Unknown Sailors' Cemetery." The legislation described the tract that would be dedicated to the burial site, and it was identical to the property that the town of Lewes had leased to the Menhaden Company of Reedville, Virginia. The proposed memorial became popularly known as the "Tomb of the Unknown Sailor," echoing the Tomb of the Unknown Soldier that had been completed in Arlington National. A report in the Delaware attorney general office concluded, "In Washington, we have a splendid monument to the Unknown Soldier, and, while the sailors buried here in Lewes were not heroes of war, [t]hey also died doing their Duty."[148]

The law delegated to the Delaware Society for the Preservation of Antiquities the responsibility to restore, reconstruct, care for, and maintain the Unknown Sailors' Cemetery. The president of the society was Wilmington socialite Mary Wilson Thompson, who was an early and vocal opponent of a third factory. Thompson was not interested in a simple plaque and a memorial to the Unknown Sailor. She envisioned the entire plot enclosed with anchor chains fastened between concrete blocks. The dune covering the entire space originally leased for a fish factory would be left in its natural state enhanced with native plants and grasses. Anchors would mark the graves of the hundreds of seamen who lost their lives at sea. Her plans also called for a large striking shaft to be created by one of the nation's leading female sculptors. Such a "Tomb of the Unknown Sailor" would cost some money. The State of Delaware had not appropriated any funds when it authorized Thompson to build a memorial on the Lewes beachfront, and the Society for the Preservation of Antiquities did not have the resources. While Thompson did not want to solicit donations, she did make it clear that her organization was eager to accept them: "Such gifts of money will be exempt from taxes in accordance with the law pertaining to historical projects."[149]

Undeterred by a lack of funds, Thompson moved forward and brought together in June a planning meeting at her Rehoboth Beach home. Among the forty-plus people attending were Governor Richard C. McMullen, Chef Justice Daniel J. Layton, Attorney General James R. Morford, and State Archivist George Ryden.* After "preaching to the choir" about why the Tomb of the Unknown Sailor was right and just, the meeting turned to the legal issues. The question seemed to be whether Lewes even had the authority to lease plots on the beachfront. In 1929, the General Assembly had given the revenues from all public lands to the State Highway Commission, which on the face of it would have included the bayfront. Justice Layton questioned the right of the state legislature to manage the land that William Penn had apparently granted to the town in 1683. The meeting, with the attorney general present, decided to formally petition him for an opinion on whether Lewes had the right to lease the land and on whether Delaware had the right to authorize Thompson's organization to erect a monument on the land. Such an opinion from the attorney general would greatly influence the Court of Chancery, where Layton felt the question of control of the Lewes beachfront would ultimately be answered.[150]

The legal issue indeed went back to 1683, when William Penn granted Edmund Warner most of Cape Henlopen. The remaining land, or bayfront, would "forever hereafter lye [sic] in common for the use of the inhabitants of the Town of Lewes and the County of Sussex." When Warner died without an heir, the town assumed administration and control of Cape Henlopen and the bayfront for over two hundred years without challenge until, that is, a cemetery for the unknown sailors was used to stop the construction of the third menhaden plant. A prominent Georgetown attorney, Houston Wilson, asked Attorney General Morford for an opinion on the legality of the lease of public land considering the 1683 land grant, about which Wilson admitted he knew little. To fill this gap, Wilson urged the attorney general to fund research into the exact meaning of Penn's grant to Warner: "The grant,

---

*The news account does not list Attorney General Robert R. Morford in attendance. It is the author's contention that Morford did attend the meeting because Houston Wilson wrote in a letter to Morford, "the ancient grant by William Penn which was mentioned in our conversation concerning the above matter at the home of Mrs. Henry B. Thompson." [Houston Wilson to James M. [sic] Morford, June 29, 1939, "Lewes Sailors Cemetery, 1939-1941," Attorney General Files (RG 1650,023) Delaware Public Archives, Dover, DE.]

in whatever form it may take, seems to have a firmer foundation than pure rumor, and I feel the time has come to trace the matter to the original sources in order that the question of its existence might be settled once and for all. It would be a matter of state-wide interest." That fall, the attorney general agreed to allocate funds for Albert Cook Myers, head librarian of the Pennsylvania Historical Society, to research the Warner grant because the General Assembly had "seen fit to constitute the Delaware Society a state agency, it is our duty to assist in establishing the Society's position in the matter."[151]

To investigate the 1683 William Penn grant to Edmund Warner, the attorney general asked Myers to determine its historical background and legal significance. Health issues soon ended Myers' involvement. In his place, Houston Wilson arranged with Morford and Thompson for Leon deValinger of the Delaware Public Archives to complete the task. Houston warned that deValinger's research may take some time because of his responsibilities as assistant state archivist. Delay did not deter Thompson, who vowed to continue to carry out the General Assembly's mandate "if . . . and when the legal difficulties are straightened out." Four months later, deValinger submitted a brief nineteen-page study, "Report on the Historical Background of the 'Unknown Sailors Cemetery' Lewes, Delaware."[152]

From the perspective of those favoring the Unknown Sailor memorial, the deValinger report was a disappointment. It traced control of the Cape Henlopen area, beginning with the 1683 Warner grant and ending with an 1818 act establishing trustees for schools in Lewes. DeValinger concluded that the proprietary may not have vested the management of the Cape with the Town of Lewes. The report ended, "This search was not continued beyond the session of 1818 as it is believed that the legal status of the lands in question may be readily traced from this year to date through the published session laws of the Delaware Assembly." Wilson and Thompson did not accept deValinger's analysis, and Wilson continued the historical research into what Thompson labeled the "Title Search for the Unknown Sailor's Cemetery." In April 1941, Wilson completed his "Report on the Cape Henlopen Title" and submitted it to the attorney general. The analysis focused on the "many and varied acts of the General Assembly effecting [sic] the lands" since statehood or, in other words, picking up where deValinger had stopped. In preparation for the semi-annual meeting of the Society for the Preservation of Antiquities two months later, Thompson asked Attorney General Morford for an informal analysis of the Wilson report and its impact on the sailors' monument. He replied that he had indeed received the report but had not yet read it, warning that "it may take weeks or months." Morford promised, "I shall give this matter as much time as is compatible with my other commitments." At the society's meeting, President Thompson reported that the Wilson study was complete "but that a decision has not yet been reached by the Attorney General as to whether our Society can take possession." The attorney general never issued an opinion, nor did he explain his failure to do so.[153]

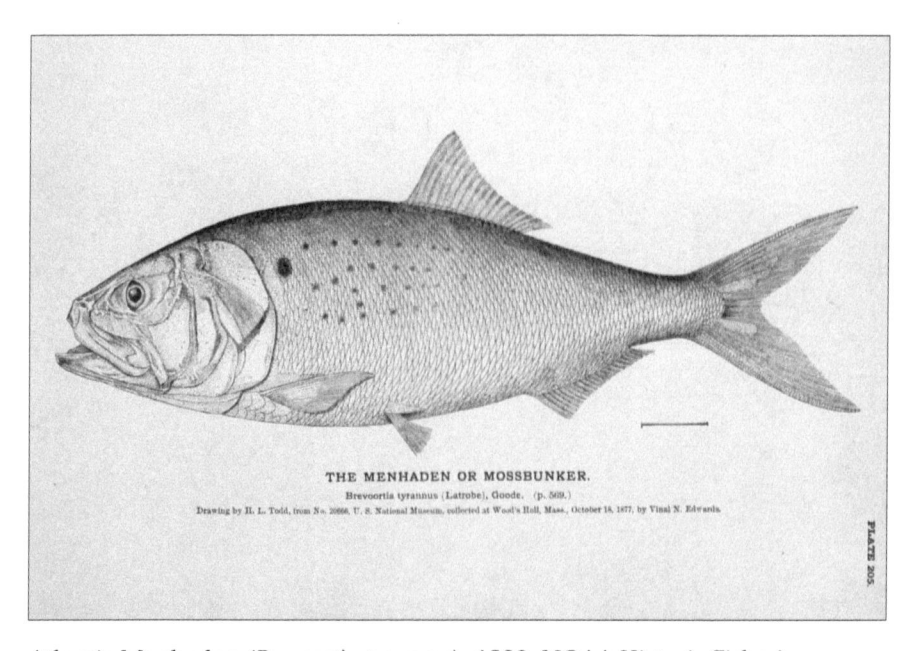

Atlantic Menhaden (*Brevoortia tyrannus*), 1880. NOAA Historic Fisheries Collection.

Purse net encircles a menhaden school, 1887. NOAA Historic Fisheries Collection.

An early menhaden vessel, *John L. Lawrence*, with a tall crow's nest, wide hull, shallow draft, and davits aft for purse boats, 1905. Lewes Historical Society.

A modern diesel-powered ship, *Princess Bay*, echoed the external design of earlier vessels, 1950. Lewes Historical Society.

Elevators lifted menhaden from fishing steamers to the pier, 1915. Delaware Public Archives.

The Fisheries Company piers and elevators, 1905. Lewes Historical Society.

Menhaden factory workers before World War I were European immigrants from Baltimore and Philadelphia supplemented by local African Americans, 1905. Lewes Historical Society.

William C. Lofland (right), most prominent menhaden entrepreneur from 1911 to 1922. Lewes Historical Society.

Consolidated Fisheries Company operated from 1922 to 1954, the longest period for any enterprise in Lewes history. ca. 1933. Delaware Public Archives.

ATTENTION! CITIZENS!

vote for
MARSHALL HAZZARD
and
EDWARD SUTHARD
for Town Commissioners

These two men are well known citizens of Lewes, Mr. Hazzard being one of the foremost political leaders in this vicinity, while Mr. Suthard, now sheriff of Sussex Co., has been one of our most successful business men. Having the support of Thomas & Richard Hayes and our local Ford dealer, Mr. Norman Baylis, they can be depended upon, if elected, to retain the two fish factories now located on Lewes Beach. To be exact they are favorable towards keeping the two factories now here, but are opposed to the third one.

It is a well known fact these factories should be kept here and not removed. Though to some extent they do pollute our air and waters. Should a few silly bathers have a right to cause their removal? Emphatically, NO!

Mr. Richard Hayes and Mr. Thomas Hayes are well known to the people of this community. They are the owners of the Consolidated Fisheries and are good employers, always paying top wages. We know it is their duty to endorse Mr. Hazzard and Mr. Suthard, who, if elecced, will protect their interests as well as those of the town.

So, Mr. and Mrs. Citizen, come out and help us elect Hazzard and Suthard. Let those who do not want the Fish Factories remove themselves and let the factories alone.

Do not forget the election is next Saturday, Jan. 7, 1939. Meet us at the polls and don't fail to vote for

HAZZARD and SUTHARD

The Friendly Five

Campaign flyer during the 1939 election whose key issue was the future of menhaden factories. Lewes Historical Society.

Watermen pull the net into the purse boats to compact the fish into a dense "bunt." Lewes Historical Society.

Power block or winches in the middle of each purse boat mechanically pack the menhaden into a tight "bunt." Lewes Historical Society.

Line of new aluminum purse boats with power block upon their arrival, 1958. Lewes Historical Society.

Workers outfit a new purse boat after its arrival, 1958. Lewes Historical Society.

Where Menhaden Was King

Driver hauls away a wooden purse boat after aluminum ones arrived, 1958. Lewes Historical Society.

Brailing net drops fish lifted from the bunt into the hold, 1930s. Lewes Historical Society.

Where Menhaden Was King

Vacuum tube drops fish sucked from the bunt into the hold, 1950s. Lewes Historical Society.

Seamen play checkers as they head into port at the end of the day, 1930s. North Carolina State Archives.

Men wrap a purse net around a net reel to dry, 1950s. Lewes Historical Society.

Net menders repair holes in purse nets and remove detritus. Lewes Historical Society.

Where Menhaden Was King

Barrington or Sater - Int. 2879

DEPARTMENT OF THE INTERIOR
INFORMATION SERVICE

FISH AND WILDLIFE SERVICE

For Release FEBRUARY 3, 1954

COMMERCIAL FISHERIES CATCH INCREASED IN 1953

The 1953 catch of commercial fish and shellfish in the United States and Alaska totaled about 4,400,000,000 pounds, as compared with 4,300,000,000 pounds in 1952, according to a report to Secretary of the Interior Douglas McKay today by John L. Farley, Director of the Fish and Wildlife Service.

The increase was due to a spectacular gain in the catch of menhaden, one of the least known but most important species of commercial fish. A substantial supply of menhaden on the Atlantic Coast and a heavy demand for menhaden meal for poultry and swine feeding were responsible for the increased landings.

The outstanding fishing port in 1953, in volume of landings, was Lewes, Del., where 360,000,000 pounds of menhaden were landed. San Pedro, Calif., which held first place for many years, was second with landings of 328,000,000 pounds principally of tuna, Pacific and Jack mackerel, and sardines.

Other leading ports for which poundage figures are available were: Gloucester, Mass., with 186,000,000 pounds mainly of ocean perch, whiting, haddock, and pollock; Boston, Mass., with 152,000,000 pounds principally of haddock, cod, pollock, whiting, ocean perch, and flounders; Reedville, Va., with 152,000,000 pounds of menhaden; and San Diego, Calif., with 128,000,000 pounds chiefly of tuna.

The outstanding ports with respect to value of the catch were San Pedro, with landings worth $32,800,000, and San Diego, with a catch valued at $20,250,000. The catch value at these two ports far outweighed other domestic ports.

x x x

P.N. 55340

Fish and Wildlife Service press release announces Lewes the nation's "outstanding fishing port" for the 1953 season. U. S. Department of Interior.

Captain Arnold C. Ripley (left), Eileen Ripley, and Otis Smith at the launch of the *Green Run*, 1962. Lewes Historical Society.

J. Howard Smith, Inc. repair and winter storage facility on the Wicomico River in Maryland. NABB Research Center, Salisbury University.

Fish Products Company (bottom) and Seacoast Products Company (top) on the Lewes bayfront, 1968. Photograph by Bobby Cubbage.

Chapter 13

A Critical Industry Survives

World War II dramatically changed the culture, society, political landscape, and economy of the United States. It brought women into the workforce, encouraged migration of African Americans from the South to the northern industrial cities, enlarged the federal government and its power, enabled millions of veterans through the GI Bill to join the middle class, and expanded home ownership through Veterans Administration loans. The waters of change also washed over the menhaden industry nationally and locally in Lewes, but it survived the flood.

For the duration of World War II, the War Production Board declared menhaden reduction a "critical industry" because of the vital need for its fish oil used in the manufacture of nitroglycerin. The board reserved one-third of the menhaden oil produced by the Lewes plants, but the government preferred pilchard and sardine oil and did not purchase all the menhaden oil it had reserved. This led J. Howard Smith to sarcastically comment, "[M]y feeling is that the Oil Division of the War Production Board is a good place to keep away from." Fish meal was another story. The nation's war machine required the flow of food, and menhaden fish meal was in great demand for swine and poultry feed. Using fish meal as a fertilizer additive had declined in the 1930s and was even prohibited during World War II. Reflective of its importance to animal feed, the secretary of agriculture demanded in 1943 a 50 percent increase in the production of fish meal for swine and poultry feed. Federal legislation was proposed in Congress to suspend all state restrictions on menhaden fishing for the duration of the war.[154]

Despite being a critical industry, the menhaden fishery faced several wartime obstacles. Factory owners remembered the government's requisition of their ocean-worthy boats in World War I. Five days after Pearl Harbor, the American Fishing Association Cooperative (AFAC), a nation-wide association of independent menhaden companies that worked together on shared problems, notified its members that there is "more likelihood" that the government will take over some menhaden vessels "because of the present emergency." In February 1942, another AFAC bulletin asked the owners of the menhaden companies to submit to the association "a list of boats that you have that you feel can readily be offered for sale or charter to the Federal Government." While the federal government had not yet issued any official request, AFAC hoped that "the requirements of the Government can be supplied from a list of boats that are not absolutely essential to the operation of the fishing industries."[155]

This fear of a government seizure of vessels proved prescient as the Coast Guard did indeed requisition the newest, best, and largest boats from fishing companies nationwide. The military acquisition had little direct impact on the Consolidated Fisheries Company of Thomas and Richard Hayes. The Hayes' fleet was aging, its newest boat having been built in 1920. With such an obsolete fleet, the Hayes operations mainly relied on boats owned by Joseph Jett's Menhaden Company and by others. In contrast, the factories of J. Howard Smith, Inc., including Fish Products in Lewes, processed fish mainly caught by ships it owned, skippered by its captains, and staffed by its employees. After expanding in the 1920s and 1930s, the Smith family had plants and ships on the Atlantic Coast stretching from Florida to New York. So, Fish Products Company was the only company with a Lewes presence whose ships were subject to seizure.[156]

While ship seizures loomed throughout the spring of 1942, the first requisition arrived at the offices of J. Howard Smith, Inc. in June, when the military asked for the transfer of three ships, including the *Promised Land*. By then, the company had outfitted the ship for the season, hired a captain, engaged a full crew, and slated the vessel for its first fishing trip of the season, which was less than a week away. Gilbert Smith lamented, "[I]t is just too late for us to in any way replace her, the PROMISED LAND." By fall, however, the military had taken control of thirteen of the thirty boats owned by the Smith companies. Of these, at least five were associated with the plant in Lewes: *Annie Daw, H. R. Humphreys, Helen Euphane, Little Joe,* and *Northumberland*. The company received no compensation because the president of Fish Products Company "feels that . . . he can well afford to contribute the services of his boats for this short period of time to the war effort in the interest of patriotism." The Coast Guard had argued that it needed these ships immediately to patrol the coastal waters during the coming winter. By

March 1943, none of the thirteen Smith ships taken by the government had been deployed for patrol. The AFAC asked for "the return of the boats not essential to the protection of the coastal areas of the United States . . . [and claimed] the urgent necessity that was apparent last fall has probably subsided." The plea to return the craft fell on deaf ears, but no additional seizures took place during the war.[157]

After losing its finest and newest vessels to the war effort, the menhaden industry nationwide revamped and pressed into service some older vessels. Many of ships were well past the sixty-year mark and had been rebuilt several times in their history. The latest refurbishing included the replacement of the original steam equipment with diesel engines. In Lewes, this meant the rejuvenation of the of *Luce Brothers* and the *John L. Lawrence*, both originally launched in 1877, and the *Sterling*, built in 1879. Coordinator of Fisheries Harold L. Ickes reported in June 1943 that these three vessels "have been coming in with solid deck loads of menhaden for the past month."[158]

Equaling the importance of ships to the menhaden industry were the men who crewed those ships or who labored in the factories processing the catches. Menhaden fishing was a labor-intensive industry. Labor shortages were felt by every economic sector throughout the country. Greater wartime production of armaments demanded millions of new jobs, while the draft reduced the number of young men available for civilian jobs. To preserve the labor force that the "arsenal for democracy" required, the employees of a wide range of businesses declared critical—including the menhaden industry—received exemptions from being drafted. Despite these deferments, patriotism motivated many workers to enlist, until September 1943 when a presidential directive prohibited the voluntary enlistment by workers in critical industries. The menhaden industry still faced a drain on its manpower. As manufacturers switched to producing planes, tanks, guns, bombs, and other instruments of war twenty-four hours a day, the higher wages they offered lured the unskilled workers from the menhaden boats and plants. Nothing prevented workers from moving from one critical industry to another, and money proved irresistible to some.[159]

Finding enough employees was not the only human resources concern. The menhaden administrators had to adapt their *laissez faire* personnel system to new governmental regulations. For example, under the Espionage Act of 1917, President Roosevelt declared a national emergency in December 1941, which required that every person working on vessels in territorial waters have an identification card issued by the U. S. Coast Guard. To obtain the card, a person had to be fingerprinted at a Coast Guard station and bring passport-sized photographs, a birth certificate, and nationalization papers or proof of alien registration. But such documentation was not always available for migrant workers. Soon, these requirements extended to employees on shore in the factories and offices as well.[160]

Every industry fell under war time wage controls. Each company had to submit to the National War Labor Board (NWLB) a position classification structure and wage range schedule, which determined pay increases. The armaments plants, many of which had unionized operations when the mobilization began, had well-established personnel systems. Neither Consolidated Fisheries nor Fish Products, however, had a job classification system or wage schedule. Fish Products admitted that its "corporation has never had a stable employment policy; that employees were recruited from whatever source available and utilized wherever possible in the operations of the plant; [and] that wage rates have never been established." The NWLB required that this void be filled. Fish Products, therefore, developed a wage scale for each job classification in its factory: $35 to $55 per week for foremen; $32 to $45 per week for their assistants; 50 cents to 75 cents per hour for semi-skilled labor; and 42 cents to 60 cents per hour for unskilled labor. Office workers were salaried but received less than the foremen and assistant foremen in the factory. A similar document was not developed for the fishermen aboard the menhaden vessels because all ships at sea were exempt from World War II wage controls.[161]

As a partial solution to the labor shortage, the federal government in 1943 began allowing essential industries to use prisoners of war. This was not possible in Delaware since it was part of the Eastern Defense Command, which prohibited the housing of enemy soldiers in proximity to the Atlantic coast. In early 1944, the labor shortage began to outweigh the potential danger of enemy soldiers near the Chesapeake and Delaware Bays, and the prohibition on POWs in Delaware was lifted.

A consortium of poultry plants, Delaware's leading agricultural industry, initiated the use of POWs in Sussex County. In June 1944, it arranged for 140 captured German soldiers to be re-assigned from Fort DuPont near Delaware City to Lewes. The POWs were placed in the former Civilian Conservation Corps camp on Savannah Road. Each day, they were transported to Rehoboth or Millsboro for work in canneries, on farms, or in a lumber mill. However, it was not until a month before V-E Day that the Lewes fish factories began to use POWs. Before any business could use a POW, it had to try to recruit labor from both inside and outside of the state and offer free housing for any laborers hired from another state. This was to ensure that a POW would not hold a job if an American worker were available. Only after recruiting failed to find employable workers could the employer sign a contract with the U.S. Army. It required the employer to use the prisoners five days a week and provide transportation each day with a guard between the camp and work site. By the end of 1945, 3,000 prisoners had been moved from Fort DuPont to support businesses throughout Sussex County. In Lewes, Fish Products Company and Consolidated Fisheries Company had about seventy-five POWs in their total onshore workforce of 700. These men held positions in the factory processing fish as well as in general labor engaged in painting, welding, and plumbing. At least two POWs worked in the Fish Products office. POWs, however, were not allowed to work on fishing vessels. Since the first POWs did not begin working until late in the war, the labor source did not significantly lessen the wartime labor shortage. Their main contribution was putting the menhaden factories on a peacetime footing before they were repatriated in 1946 and 1947.[162]

Materials, like workers, were in short supply. The federal government organized its domestic manufacturing to meet its need for tanks, small arms, machine guns, heavy bombers, aircraft engines, antiaircraft guns, and other weapons. A government bureaucracy with forms, processes, and procedures allocated limited raw resources. In competition for these resources, the menhaden industry, although a "critical industry," did not fare well. For example, J. Howard Smith, Inc. needed to purchase two diesel engines in March 1942 to refurbish older ships for the start of the fishing season in June. To get engines in time, it needed a "Triple A" priority. Instead, the engines had a priority of only "Double A," which authorized delivery in November. Similar administrative hurdles made procuring needed replacement parts for their ships and factories difficult.[163]

The menhaden industrialists even had difficulty acquiring nets. They needed hard-fiber material, such as manila and sisal, but the primary sources of these products were in Japanese hands. Competing domestically for the limited amount of these raw materials was the military, which needed high quality ropes for its naval warships, troop carriers, and merchant marine vessels. Nets themselves also proved useful for camouflage in war zones.[164]

The final obstacle to this "critical industry" was the limitations that the navy imposed on fishing in strategically significant waters. The area around the mouth of Delaware Bay was declared off limits to fishing vessels because the bay provided access to munition factories and oil refineries to the north. Steamers from Lewes were also banned near the mouth of the Chesapeake Bay because of its proximity to major naval facilities. In both areas, the menhaden vessels could pass through but could not engage in fishing operations. To the disadvantage of the menhaden business, these were some of the finest fishing grounds. Despite these restrictions, Coordinator of Fisheries Harold L. Ickes commented, "Exceptionally good runs of fish, combined with the efforts of the industry to meet the unprecedented demands for its products, are believed to have made possible this year's [1943] large catches, in spite of the fact that the fishery is operating with a reduced fleet and is barred from of the best fishing areas by Naval restrictions."[165]

Even with the war effort officially needing fish meal and fish oil from the Lewes menhaden plants, the U.S. Army surprisingly filed in June 1943 a federal lawsuit to close Consolidated Fisheries. The Army argued that the fish odor was so objectionable to the servicemen at a nearby military base on Cape Henlopen that it was impeding the war effort. The Army said that the waste from the factories bred flies that swarmed the soldiers' housing and mess halls thus threatening their health. Substantiating how noxious the odor was, the legal brief claimed that some soldiers had to resort to gas masks while others had become so nauseated that they were unable to eat. Rejecting such drastic action, U.S. District Judge Paul Leahy enjoined the fisheries to decrease "giving off of offensive and noisome odors or the breeding of flies, maggets [sic], and vermin at their factory at Lewes." Consolidated Fish Factories bought additional deodorizing equipment and pledged in October that the foul conditions had been corrected.[166]

With the celebrations of V-E and V-J Days in 1945, America's manufacturers that had converted from producing durable consumer goods to munitions and weapons of war needed to revert to their former missions. Lewes' menhaden industry, like its counterparts in agriculture and other industries, had not changed its pre-war output. It had not prospered and grown as some other industries nor had it collapsed like others. It survived.

CHAPTER 14

Organizing the Smith Companies

J.Howard and Gilbert Smith's first business, before World War I, was an informal partnership between two brothers. After World War II and coinciding with their time in Lewes, they transformed this partnership into a corporation with numerous subsidiaries. As a result, J. Howard Smith, Inc. became the largest menhaden reduction business in the country, producing 65 percent of the nation's fish meal and fish oil. The company managed every step: catching fish with its ships, processing them in its factories using its employees, and selling products through its marketing wing. In 1950, the corporation not only established a repair and winter storage facility for its ships on the Wicomico River in Maryland, to avoid relying on outside vendors for repairs. One subsidiary was even dedicated to research and development. The Smiths carefully organized their companies; now the unions wanted to organize the workers.[167]

The Lewes menhaden factories were a cog in the much larger Smith family organization. In the mid-1950s, the Smith menhaden operation consisted of six companies, each operating a fish plant, including the two in Lewes—Fish Products and Seacoast Products. While the production companies owned the factories, they did not own the fishing vessels (another Smith subsidiary owned those). Other corporate entities marketed products for all the factories and operated airplanes to search for menhaden schools. Each company was a totally owned subsidiary of J. Howard Smith, Inc. with its headquarters in Port Monmouth, New Jersey.

The five children of J. Howard Smith—Harvey Ward Smith, Otis Smith, Mary Gladys Smith Cubbage, Gilbert Porter Smith II, and Janice M. Smith Clarke—owned equal shares of J. Howard Smith, Inc. and each subsidiary. However, while the brothers and sisters each owned equal shares, the factories and ancillary corporations operated independently under the direction of one male family member who was designated president: Otis and Harvey; Mary's husband, C.M. "Pete" Cubbage; and Janice's husband, Larry I. Clarke. Nationwide, each Smith factory competed with the company's other factories for the most fish landed and the most money made. A chronicler of the menhaden industry, John Frye, commented: "At one time, the companies, linked by joint family ownership but each managed competitively—even against each other—by a family, accounted for 65 percent of the country's catch of menhaden and production of fish oil and fish meal." Enhancing the family enterprise, the remaining slots for corporate officers and board directors were nominally filled by other family members, including the women. Otis Smith was the president of the two Delaware production companies, Fish Products Company and Seacoast Products Company, and as president ran both companies without interference from the others. While all five siblings equally owned the companies, Otis Smith appeared the first among equals. Harvey Smith, however, would probably disagree with that assessment.[168]

The competition between Harvey Smith and his younger brother, Otis, may have been especially intense since they were so close in age, less than two years apart. They attended Washington and Lee University one year apart and were members of Sigma Phi Epsilon, a social fraternity. After his undergraduate work, Harvey attended Pace Institute in New York City to study accounting and became a certified public account. At the direction of his father, he immediately moved to Beaufort to build a menhaden factory and remained there until he passed away in 1976.[169]

Although the presidents of the production companies ran their factories without interference from the other siblings, they did not own the ships that supplied the fish. Another J. Howard Smith, Inc. subsidiary did. The Atlantic Navigation Company, in 1953, assumed ownership of the Smith family's entire fleet of menhaden steamers, handling payroll, compliance, withholdings, and other clerical activities. The centralized paperwork freed the captains to devote their energies to catching menhaden.

At the beginning of each season, the captains and the Atlantic Navigation Company developed a written "charter" or contract that made them independent contractors and that included a fish purchase agreement. Since the captains took directions from the president of the factory, though, they felt like a "factory owner" had "hired" them. The captains then hired their crews, with most returning year after year. While much of the menhaden processed through a Smith factory were caught by Smith ships, Smith plants occasionally bought fish directly from captains who owned their own vessels.

The captains retained control over the means and manner of the daily fishing operation, from the time to start, to whether it would start at all, to where the ship would fish. Each captain and his crew competed with the other boats, striving to be the season's "high boat" or the ship that landed the most fish. This was important financially, because the bonuses were determined by the number of fish caught, as well as psychologically, because the "high boat" had bragging rights.[170]

Such a major industry with a large labor force of seamen and factory workers became a prime target for union organizers. The first two attempts to unionize were unsuccessful, both in 1936 at Reedville, Virginia, and in 1952 at the Smith family's operation in Port Monmouth, New Jersey. In the latter, five union organizers were arrested, charged by local authorities with trespassing, and escorted out of town. Meanwhile, African American fishermen on the Smith company boats in Virginia designated to supply the Fish Products factory in Lewes went on strike. The company replaced these striking workers, in part, by hiring College of William & Mary football players for the summer.[171]

By 1956, the attempts to unionize resumed as the International Brotherhood of Teamsters appropriated $500,000 to organize non-union workers in areas that included Lewes. Otis Smith and some of the other family members realized that the unionization of the menhaden workers was "inevitable" and felt that an agreement with a union that "is a reasonably reputable conservative organization" could be constructive. Their belief that "a measure of cooperation with the union's organizational efforts" could result in "future amiable relations with the union." They hoped that such cooperation would result in "a somewhat unobnoxious [sic] long-term contract." Not all Smith family members shared this willingness to negotiate with a union for a favorable contract; Harvey Smith was opposed to any union. All family members probably agreed on one point: it would be ultimately impractical to have contracts for the vessels and not have contracts for onshore factories. According to a Smith labor attorney, "[When] one becomes organized, the organization of the other cannot be far away." Despite this perception, the initial union contracts concerned only the crew on the fishing vessels.[172]

Otis Smith, representing the Smith companies, had three meetings in August 1956 with Harry Poole and Melvin Tyler of the Amalgamated Meat Cutter and Butcher Workmen of North America's Union. In the first meeting, Smith took a hard line, and somewhat erroneously claimed that "we have had drives by unions before which always resulted in violence and generally unbearable conditions and that we are, on the strength of our previous experiences, very strongly opposed to unions." He quickly softened his position by adding, "we realize that there are probably unions operated by decent people in which case we would not be so strongly opposed to such a union as we were to previous unions dominated by Communistic influences." He described the second meeting a week later as "very amiable" and expressed that he "personally would not be opposed to the unions." During the third meeting three weeks later, Smith's brothers-in-law, Cubbage and Clarke, joined the negotiations. Smith volunteered that he had called businessmen outside of the menhaden enterprise that negotiated with the union and "was very pleasantly surprised to learn what he [the union representative] had told us about his reputation was quite true." Those companies, Smith continued, "seemed very pleased with the union agents and all in all appeared to be satisfied with union."[173]

The sticking point in the negotiations was the legal status of the captain and his boat. Each captain was an independent contractor who chartered a boat from Atlantic Navigation and who employed the watermen. The crew, therefore, had no relationship with J. Howard Smith, Inc. The negotiations centered on figuring out a system of union contracts that would acknowledge this technicality. While both sides shared the same goal, they could not discern a legal path. The last meeting that year ended with an agreement that the union's attorneys would contact the Smith companies' attorneys.[174]

In spring of the following year, Thomas M. Kerrigan, the Smith attorney for labor matters, felt that negotiations with the union should not continue. With any additional talks, he said, the "Union would justly be entitled to believe that the conference and negotiations were in good faith leading to a contract." Since no one representing the captains was involved in the conferences, the negotiations appeared to have been conducted on behalf of the entire company. The attorney feared that the National Labor Relations Board would, if the union secured enough signatures for an election, determine that "the entire fleet of each company to be an appropriate collective bargaining unit." In such a case, a labor dispute would not be limited to a single boat but could involve the entire fleet of every Smith factory. Kerrigan warned, "To be able to tie up an entire fleet as compared to one vessel places the

Union in a much better bargaining position."[175]

Since Otis Smith had the best relationship with the union, the other family members asked him to communicate that the Smith companies were withdrawing from the talks. Smith said that "other stockholders," referring to his brother Harvey, were so opposed to his effort that he was "in an embarrassing position with respect to his associates." Also, he asserted that "many of the captains have objected to the fact that he has inserted himself into their business affairs unnecessarily." In short, Otis Smith explained that he no longer wanted to be "in the intermediary position he has taken." Although the discussions between the Smith companies and the union dissolved, the labor organizers would be permitted on "a reasonable basis" to negotiate with each captain. This strategy was essentially a "delaying tactic" so that it would take longer for the union to organize and thus enable the companies to "get through the entire present season before they [union representatives] can bring things to a head."[176]

Labor negotiations for an agreement covering the fishermen did indeed come to a head the following year. The attorneys found a way to insulate the individual boats from forming a corporate fleet for contract purposes: create a separate corporation for each vessel, with the captain its chief operating officer. Labor negotiations are always easier in prosperous times, and 1958 was part of the boom years of record landings, particularly in Lewes. The captains were paid for each pound of menhaden landed, and the crew worked for a flat hourly wage and a bonus for each pound landed. The captains and the crew were doing quite well financially. The corporate-wide installation of new equipment, such as the power block, on all the boats had cut the number of fishermen in half from the previous year. This allowed each worker to earn more income in the 1958 season because the pie did not need to be cut in as many slices. As Otis Smith told his workers at the start of the season, "[Y]ou should understand that the power block and the reduction in the number of the men in the crew is for your benefit as well as the Company's benefit. As partners, we will share the benefits."[177]

That September, Otis Smith successfully negotiated a contract with the Amalgamated Meat Cutters Union, agreeing that a standard contract "with same conditions for all" boats would be signed by the corporation that owned a specific boat and by the fishermen on that boat. The union leaders would explain its advantages to the men, while Smith agreed to explain to the captains why this was beneficial from the management's perspective. The captains were indifferent to a union contract. They only asked that crew members had to have permission before they could leave the ship; that all crew members would serve as net menders; that engine men must be mechanics; that every man must stay on board during the stormy season; that employees could be fired for "sloppy work"; and that the boats be permitted to fish six days a week. The agreement either explicitly contained each of these provisions or left them as conditions that would be negotiated each year before the season. The contract also avoided a discussion of pay and share rates, merely agreeing that they would likewise be negotiated annually.[178]

The contract guaranteed job security by stipulating that all men would be called back for the next season unless notified thirty days before the end of the season with an explanation. If the employee appealed such a notification, the company and the union would "jointly" investigate. In cases of disputes between the union and management, binding arbitration would involve the Federal Board of Mediation along with the understanding that, "While grievances are being processed, all work will go on as usual." The agreement also contained Otis Smith's priority that there "shall be no authorized strike or stoppage of work by the Union." This no-strike clause was balanced with a management promise not to lock out any employee. Furthermore, the companies promised that there "shall be no discrimination against any employee because of race, color, creed, age or nationality." The first contracts covered the period from April 1, 1959 to March 31, 1960. The fishermen receiving lodging in a bunk house and food in the mess hall were paid $1.10 per hour and fishermen not receiving lodging and food were paid $1.40 per hour. These wages had the added benefit of overtime and were supplemented by the watermen's "share." Otis Smith was later able to replace arbitration with mediation in exchange for stipulating that all watermen had to join the union and that union dues would be deducted from the employees' checks. The fishermen strongly objected to the latter provision; but, the contract had to be enforced, and the Smith companies' attorney made clear his position: "This means that if any fisherman refuses to pay dues he must be discharged."[179]

Almost as soon as the ink was dry, the contracts began to unravel when the companies' profitability declined. At the start of the 1960 season, fourteen captains signed a petition stating that they "are *not* [original emphasis] willing to fish the 1960 season for less than 60 cents per thousand [pounds]." The companies agreed to the increase in pay that the captains received for each catch. Negotiations continued each year because the captains wanted a larger cut despite the companies losing money. As the losses continued, the company began to stop using some of the vessels. Under the structure in which each vessel was a separate corporation, the captain as a corporate officer was not eligible for unemployment compensation. To remedy this, in 1963, a new corporation for each ship was formed with the principal officers being the companies' labor attorney and an accountant. In turn, each corporation hired a captain, making him an employee and thus eligible for unemployment insurance. This structure preserved the crew of each ship as a separate bargaining unit.[180]

These contracts covered only the fishermen and omitted the other personnel aboard the ships, such as first mates and engineers. The engineers were demanding an increase in pay because they had more machinery to maintain as automation had replaced manual laborers. The engineers claimed that "manual labor of the fishermen [is] practically non-existent" in this "mechanical nightmare of electronics, hydraulics, and engines." Into this environment, the Inland Boatmen's Union of the Seafarers International Union claimed that a majority of the first mates, pilots, and engineers aboard the twenty-one vessels operating out of Lewes had signed cards for the union to represent them. The Smith companies feared this because the "group comprises the management of each boat" and unionizing them "could be fatal to the operation." When the petition was invalidated and the Seafarers Union learned that each boat needed to be organized separately, it gave up on organizing these workers. In contrast, the Amalgamated Meat Cutters Union expanded its effort in the menhaden industry when it secured in 1963 signed cards from most of the factory workers in the two factories in Lewes. That fall, a separate union contract covered all production and maintenance employees in both Lewes factories, except for clerical staff, guards, watchmen, foremen, and supervisors.[181]

With these various contracts, in short, Smith family's Fish Products Company and Seacoast Products Company in Lewes were independent companies in an intricate organization of entities.

Chapter 15

Research and Development

Development of technological modernizations enabled the spectacular growth of menhaden landings in Lewes and elsewhere in the country. When J. Howard Smith, Inc. acquired Atlantic Fisheries in 1938, the president of the new corporation, Otis Smith, indicated that he wanted to renovate the old factory, which dated to the early 1930s. But World War II restrictions on materials and laborers postponed that until V-J Day. Similarly, when the Smith family acquired Consolidated Fisheries in 1953, Otis Smith set about modernizing factories with the latest advancements in reduction processing and in state-of-the-art steel ships equipped with diesel engines. "With Smith's 'extensive alternations' to his new acquisition," the local newspaper correctly forecasted that "an even larger number of fish are expected to be landed in Lewes and processed at the two adjoining factories."[182]

The 1950s saw the development and adoption of innovative techniques and technologies. Probably the first postwar modernization was a type of vacuum hose that Fish Products and Consolidated Fisheries adopted immediately after World War II. Fish companies elsewhere had been using hoses to suck the menhaden from a vessel's hold to a conveyor belt leading to the factory. The original system used a metal rigid pipe connected to a vacuum pump. A flexible rubber hose then replaced the metal one. The new hose was easier to manipulate in the hold, weighed less and thus was easier to work, and swayed with the boat. The pliable hoses could pull about one million fish every two hours and cut the number of men needed to unload the steamers from between eighty and ninety to between ten and twelve. This efficiency in the late 1950s prompted the fish companies to install pumps with pliable rubber hoses on the boats to fill the holds from the nets.[183]

The fish companies replaced their organic nets, made of cotton, linen or sisal, with nylon ones. The new cords were stronger, making it more difficult for the heavier schools to "blow" through the seine. Nylon was resistant to mold and mildew, which weakened the fabric nets so that even some small schools could break through. Since nylon was also lighter, the depth of the net was increased from 80 feet to 100 feet, which prevented fish from escaping over the top of the nets.[184]

A major technological breakthrough was the "power block." One of the most labor-intensive aspects of menhaden fishing was tightening a school of fish into the "bunt." In 1958, a hydraulic power block placed in the middle of each purse boat pulled the net onto the boats, thus mechanizing the creation of the bunt. What used to require fifteen to seventeen men to accomplish was reduced to eight. Initially, the first power blocks pulled the nets into the wooden purse boats, but the weight of the power blocks often pulled down the gunwales and swamped the boats. In Lewes, the purse boats were redesigned as diesel-powered aluminum craft. This change reduced the weight of each purse boat from 8400 pounds to 7200 pounds and kept the boats totally afloat even with the power blocks.[185]

The innovation with the greatest impact was probably "air spotting," or trying to locate the schools of menhaden from an airplane rather than from the crow's nest of the vessel. The effort started neither in Lewes nor in the 1950s, however. In 1920, the naval station in Norfolk teamed up with a Virginia concern to test fish spotting as a training exercise. The planes were not reliable, could not go more than 100 miles from Norfolk, and always had to remain in sight of land. The spotters could communicate with the fishing boats only after they returned to base and could send the locations to the fishing vessels in Morse code using the then state-of-the-art wireless. This effort lasted only one season since the cost deterred the industry from continuing it. In 1943, the navy resurrected air spotting on the West Coast for pilchard fishing. As part of the war effort to increase pilchard landings, the navy began using blimps to spot the fish. The positions of concentrated pilchard were radioed to shore, and the fishing vessels set sail to the areas that the spotters had located. This effort lasted through the end of World War II. Air spotting arrived on the East Coast early in the postwar period when a Nantucket pilot tried to communicate with the fishing vessels by dropping notes in a bottle to be retrieved by a skiff. These early efforts indicated the need for instantaneous voice communication between the spotter and the captain to allow this way of locating fish to reach its full potential.[186]

Otis Smith learned about successful air spotting in North Carolina,

Where Menhaden Was King

where the family had a factory. His first effort was to send a Smith-owned plane with a pilot and experienced fisherman to locate schools of menhaden. The plane returned with the information to be used by the fishing steamers twenty-four hours later, but often the fish had moved before the vessels arrived. He soon utilized planes equipped with voice radios for direct communication with the steamers. By 1955, Smith was using six radio-equipped planes to spot for boats providing raw fish to both of his Lewes factories. Over time, the pilots were replaced with experienced menhaden men, eliminating the need for a second person in the cockpit. The doors of the plane were clear glass, so the fish were visible from every angle. After finding a school of fish, the spotter pilot guided the ships to the menhaden, hovered over the area, and instructed the purse boats as they encircled the school. When the nets were in place for the maximum catch, the pilot would tell the boats to drop the "tom" weight and close the net.[187]

Lewes was not the first in air spotting, but it was on the cutting edge of scientific research into menhaden. The first effort occurred when Warren S. Schneller, a teacher at Lewes High School, put together in the late 1940s a temporary laboratory in the school's basement. The University of Delaware wanted L. Eugene Cronin, an associate professor of biology, to set up a marine laboratory in Lewes, so he joined with Schneller. Together they examined the condition of the water in the Delaware Bay and surveyed the catch of commercial fishery vessels. Their venture expanded into the University of Delaware Marine Laboratory, with an appropriation from the state secured by the combined effort of the Middle Atlantic States Fisheries Commission; M. Haswell Pierce, a member of the Commission; and Otis Smith. While engaging in a wide variety of marine studies, it did not neglect the menhaden. The Marine Laboratory expanded into the laboratory of the University of Delaware's Department of Biological Science which would subsequently become the university's College of Marine Studies in Lewes.[188]

More significant to the menhaden industry was Otis Smith's sponsorship of research and development. J. Howard Smith, Inc. underwent a major reorganization in 1953 and formed the Smith Research and Development Corporation. It was initiated by Otis Smith, headquartered in Lewes, and virtually indistinguishable from Fish Products. From the outset, research took place on a dedicated vessel at sea. Smith's first research ship was a refurbished German minesweeper purchased as war surplus. Renamed *Salisbury*, this ocean-going ship had a staff of ten scientists. A decade later, the Smith Research and Development Company launched a new research vessel, *Cape May*. One of the scientists on the ship was the German Conradin Kreutzer, whose studies were based on the theory that fish communicate with each other through electrical impulses that attracted other fish. Smith enticed Kreutzer to emigrate from Hamburg to the United States and to apply his theories to commercial fishing.[189]

Kreutzer first experimented with "electro-trawling," or pulling a net behind a trawler and trying to lure fish by electrical impulses on each side of the net's mouth. When this failed, Kreutzer and his researchers began to experiment with other applications in "electro-fishing." They succeeded when electrodes were placed at the mouth of the vacuum tube in the purse seine. The electrode enticed the menhaden to swim toward it and into the hose. This increased the efficiency of pumping the menhaden haul from the purse seine into the hold. Trying to expand on this success, the researchers hoped that the electrical impulse could be set for any size or type of fish to lure them into any size or type of net. Kreutzer was not successful, despite more than $500,000 that Otis Smith invested into his activities.[190]

Another area of research involved experimenting with a French process to reduce menhaden into fish meal containing 85 percent protein for human consumption, a pet project of Otis Smith. Co-located in Lewes and in Tuckerton, New Jersey, the pilot production effort caused the menhaden industry nation to seek the Food and Drug Administration (FDA) approval of menhaden fish meal, called "fish protein concentrate," for human consumption. Despite support from the Bureau of Commercial Fisheries in the Fish and Wildlife Service, the government in 1960 rejected the proposal because the fish meal was "adulterated," meaning that it came from the entire fish and contained all internal organs. An effort to override the agency's ruling by federal statute likewise failed. The FDA did reverse its position in 1967 and approved fish meal for human consumption domestically, but the prospect of an additional market for menhaden did not help Lewes since its factories had already closed.[191]

CHAPTER 16

The Future Looked Promising

By mid-century, the Lewes menhaden enterprise had solidified its place in the fishing industry; it was the leader in developing technology that increased catches and expedited processing, while in some years hauling more tonnage than any port in the country. One Midwestern newspaper, the *Newark Advocate*, described it in 1959: "The industry is big and getting bigger." The future looked promising, but it was not to be. Beginning in 1959, the same year as the *Advocate's* prediction, the demand for fish meal declined nationwide. New sources of fish products emerged and challenged the Atlantic factories to further depressed prices. As a result, the price for menhaden products tanked and, within three years, the landings on the Lewes fish piers shrank dramatically.[192]

From 1959 through 1962, the Lewes fish factories were apparently booming as the extraordinary landings continued. Although the last year that Lewes was the largest fishing port in the country was 1956, the annual tonnage landed remained well above 200 million pounds for the next six years and kept Lewes the nation's second-busiest fishing port. The landings began dropping nationwide in 1963, and in Lewes by half or barely 100 million pounds. This abrupt and spectacular drop caused a decline in the total commercial fish catch of all species across the country. The U.S. Interior Department lamented that this country-wide fall was "primarily due to greatly reduced landings of menhaden." When the Lewes landings did not improve in 1964, Otis Smith cut the operation in mid-summer and sent nineteen of his thirty-six fishing vessels to winter storage in Maryland. In August, he sent the remaining vessels and shuttered both fish factories. Smith attributed the decline to cold surface waters near land and much warmer water thirty miles offshore, noting that the last time fishing halted in midseason was in 1948 when the same cold-water phenomenon occurred. A storm reversed those conditions when it churned up the ocean and brought back the warm water, allowing Smith to order his vessels back to work. Optimistically, Smith commented that periods of poor menhaden landings normally lasted for only one season, except for the longest run of bad fishing that lasted four years, 1931-1934.* Despite misgivings about the return of the menhaden in 1964, Smith reopened operations in late August with only a third of his fleet "just to see what would happen."[193]

After two seasons with only 100 million pounds of landings, Otis Smith announced that Seacoast Products Company would not open in 1965 but that the other factory, Fish Products, would. While the Lewes tonnage in 1964 was comparable to the prior year, it dropped by half in 1965 to less than 50 million. The following year's landings may have been the worst since 1883 and, in the middle of the 1966 season, Smith closed Fish Products saying, "Fish are almost nonexistent." More ominous, Smith warned that the plant may not open the next year, fearing that the factory shutdown may last years and would possibly be permanent. The inescapable fact is that the Lewes menhaden fishing industry had ended its eighty-three-year history.[194]

Otis Smith continued to express his faith that the menhaden would return to the mid-Atlantic. When he announced the closing of the Seacoast plant, Smith predicted, "They'll be back." Two years later, Smith pledged that he would reopen the Fish Products plant: "Fish are scarce now, but that will change as everything in nature does." In 1967, he said that the Lewes operations "will" reopen when the fish return. The following year he backtracked somewhat and said he "wants" to reopen. As late as February 1968, Smith hoped to open his plants: "The fish go south for the winter, and until they come back, we don't know whether they are coming back. . . . We will just have to wait to find out." Despite his convictions, his attention was moving elsewhere. After the announcement that the Seacoast Plant would not open for the 1965 season, Smith transferred the plant's vessels and factory equipment to Intracoastal City, Louisiana. There, thirteen miles south of Abbeville, he opened the last fish reduction plant his family would build.[195]

"Where Did the Menhaden Go?" asked *Time* magazine. Marine biologists did not have an answer to what caused the steep drop in Lewes landings from 404 million pounds in 1956 to 50 million pounds in less than a decade. When the initial plant closure occurred in 1964, the

---

*Smith said the period of poor fishing lasted four years, starting in 1926. Contemporary sources indicate this four-year period was 1931-1934.

press reported, "Federal biologists have been called on to find out why the fish have disappeared from local waters but haven't pinpointed the reason yet." Editorially, a Maryland newspaper commented:

> Marine biologists say the disappearance of fish may be caused by changes in ocean currents, cold water and other factors. . . . Whatever the causes, and over-fishing could be a factor . . . marine biologists say they know that in the case of menhaden, not enough fish are being spawned to replace those caught.

The laboratory of the Bureau of Commercial Marine Fisheries in Beaufort, North Carolina, had studied the menhaden for years, and its head commented that they did not know enough about the fish to provide a reason for the disappearance. It was three years after the collapse of menhaden fishery when the Atlantic States Marine Commission announced that state and federal biologists were conducting joint studies into the decrease of menhaden catches. Similarly, in congress, legislators waited until 1968 to urge an appropriation of $350,000 to determine why the menhaden industry is "already in the depths of a horrendous decline."[196]

The lack of scientific explanation is understandable. Until 1963 and the first noticeable drop in the number of menhaden in the ocean, the landings were booming and presented no problems for marine biologists to investigate. The Smith Research and Development Company, based in Lewes, conducted what little scientific study of the menhaden fishery there was, and its focus was on finding more efficient methods to catch and process the fish. It was not until 1966 that the federal Sea Grant Program began funding research in marine biology at universities.[197]

Not to minimize an 80 percent drop in landings within ten years, the raw numbers may have presented a more drastic upheaval than what really happened in nature. According to Fred June, a Fish and Wildlife Service marine biologist who had studied the menhaden, the Atlantic menhaden experienced "strong *natural* fluctuations" [emphasis added]. After the menhaden spawn one or two miles out in the ocean, the hatched eggs float with the tidal waves and ocean currents toward the shore. Predators can devour the larvae, and the unpredictable changes in ocean temperatures, sudden storms, and widely changing currents lessen the chances of survival. Only an infinitesimal remnant of the eggs survives the journey to their estuarial nursery, where larvae mature after nine months into adult menhaden that will join a migrating school in the ocean. If a large number survive the treacherous journey to an estuary and the maturing of larvae into juveniles is not diminished, then a large, strong "year class" is the result. Fewer larvae reaching the estuary or maturing into adults there, for whatever reasons, will produce a small, weak "year class." The erratic survivorship of specific year classes explains the wildly cyclical nature of the size of the Atlantic menhaden fishery. June concluded, "Several unusually abundant year-classes appeared in succession [in the early 1950s]. These, together with many older fish, representing many age-groups, resulted in record yields during the greater part of the decade." The numbers in the 1950s were probably a high point of the natural fluctuations, while the devasting numbers in the mid-1960s may have been a low point.[198]

Using landings as a measurement of the number of menhaden in the ocean was also somewhat deceptive. In the boom years before 1963, the menhaden industry in Lewes used every ship and every employee to catch every fish that could be caught. When the menhaden landings dropped to 100 million pounds in 1963 and 1964, Smith's plants were not operating full time. No fish were landed in Lewes during the two-week period in the middle of the 1964 season when the factories were temporarily shuttered. In 1965, when only one plant operated, the number of ships hauling in fish was cut nearly in half, reducing the possible landings. And in 1966, the remaining plant operated for half the season, again cutting in half what might have been landed. By reducing the number of ships searching the ocean's surface for schools of menhaden, the Lewes fish companies were not catching, and thus not landing, every fish that could have been caught. So, data on landing is a useful tool but not an exact measurement of the menhaden population.

Although landings can overestimate the changes in the menhaden population that naturally fluctuates, the number of menhaden in the ocean did drop and dropped significantly. Overfishing is frequently offered as *the* explanation for the decrease. However, *National Geographic* explained that "overfishing is simply the taking of wildlife from the sea at rates too high for fished species to replace themselves." In other words, "overfishing" involves both the fishermen removing too many fish and the fish reproducing too few. Without question, the fishermen clearly did increase the landings as menhaden fishing became more efficient in the 1950s. Plane spotting found more fish more quickly; nylon nets enabled larger schools to be caught; power blocks and vacuum tubes accelerated loading the fish into the holds and transferring them to the factories. More fish in less time.[199]

Overfishing sometimes implies that companies exploit ocean wildlife. But not so with the Lewes menhaden industry. Due to the activities of Smith Research and Development Corporation, J. Howard Smith, Inc. received the "highest award the Department of Interior can bestow for conservation achievement." In presenting the Conservation Service Award, Secretary Stewart Udall noted that the company had rendered distinguished service in the cause of preservation" and specifically mentioned that it had made available a research vessel to permit the first systematic hydrographic survey of the continental shelf along the coast of New Jersey. The award to the Smith business marked the first time that a commercial fishing operator had received the prestigious award. No mention was made of whether J. Howard Smith, Inc. operated it's menhaden fishing business in an environmentally responsible manner, but it is doubtful that the Department of the Interior would recognize a company that was even suspected of irresponsible practices. In accepting the award, Otis Smith commented, "We, as commercial fishermen, are of necessity conservationists."[200]

If Fish Products Company, Seacoast Products Company, and the other Smith fishing companies on the Atlantic coast did not intentionally overfish, they sometimes did employ "selective fishing." Beginning in 1960, fish factories tried to locate the menhaden schools with the highest possible oil yield. The catch in the southern part of the Atlantic fishery south of Delaware tended to be younger and contained relatively less oil, while north of Delaware Bay the fish were older, fatter, and yielded more oil. Veteran menhaden fishermen knew this and concentrated their boats farther north for the older fish. Since the menhaden do not reach sexual maturity until the second or third year, concentrating on older fish because of their oil content netted a disproportionate number of sexually mature fish capable of replenishing the stock.[201]

The other half of the overfishing equation was the lack of replacement fish. To answer this, the Wilmington *News Journal* wondered editorially: "The causes of the dearth of menhaden? Nobody seems to know." In suggesting several explanations, the editorial raised the issue of the degradation of the estuaries where menhaden larvae mature into adults. This pollution of the bays and sounds also reflected a concern expressed in the late 1950s at the height of the menhaden catches by Fred June. He labeled an estuary as "entirely kinetic" because the slope of the basins, drainage, tides, sunlight, temperature, wind, and rainfall all "fluctuate around mean conditions." Yet "a productive aquatic environment" is maintained because these "influences tend to balance one another quite well." June warned that human activities "are a striking exception. When he, at any time, alters the inherent balance of the estuary, he can never be quite certain of the results." And June warned about the changes to the bays, inlets, and sounds caused by dredging, marsh or wetlands drainage, impoundments, recreational developments, and pollution: "Changes wrought in the estuary by such activities are often subtle, and it becomes especially difficult to measure both their immediate and long-term effect."[202]

More than a decade later, Kent S. Price Jr., a marine biologist at the University of Delaware, analyzed the Lewes menhaden industry for the Delaware Academy of Sciences. His conclusion, arguing that degradation of the estuarine nursery was one of three reasons for the demise of Delaware's menhaden fishery along with fluctuations and overfishing, meshed with June's. According to Maryland Department of Environment, the leading cause of this degradation was excess nutrient pollution. In the Chesapeake Bay and its tributaries, the decline began in the 1950s and continued through the 1960s until it reached the point that aquatic life was rapidly disappearing from the bay. More recent studies have pointed to nitrogen and phosphorous, whether they came from fertilizers lavishly deposited on farm acreage, golf courses and urban/suburban lawns, or from industrialized swine and poultry operations. Any number of these environmental changes could be lethal to the fragile embryonic menhaden that had survived the harrowing passage into the estuary. These explanations suggest that man-made pollution of the bays and other estuaries reduced the number of fish reproduced in the overfishing equation. Thus, in addition to the belief that fishermen landed too many fish, the polluted tidal waters prevented the juveniles from maturing and replacing the menhaden being harvested.[203]

In hindsight, the height of the Lewes menhaden industry was not 1956 with the largest landing of fish, nor did its decline start in 1963 with the precipitous drop in landings. The peak came in 1959 when 250 million pounds were landed. While the tonnage was less than in earlier years, sales for the catch were more than any other year in the decade. The value exceeded $75 million and included 122,000 tons of fish meal, twenty-one million gallons of oil, and 102 million gallons of fish solubles, which is a syrup leftover from the reduction process.[204]

In the four months after the 1959 fishing season, the prevailing price for poultry fell by 40 percent and the price for hogs by 30 percent. This caused animal farmers to reduce their poultry and swine inventories which, in turn, prompted a decline in the demand for fish meal and fish solubles as major additives to animal feed. At the same time two new sources of the supply of fish meal and fish solubles emerged. The first came from the Gulf of Mexico menhaden fishery, which started in the 1940s and grew during the 1950s to surpass Atlantic landings in 1963 and become the country's largest commercial fishery. The second came from other countries, particularly Peru. In 1954, Peru had produced only 24,000 tons of processed fish meal, but this markedly increased to 365,000 tons in 1959 and to over 500,000 in 1960. The output from Peruvian fish factories began to outpace that of the United States, which produced 307,000 tons of fish meal in 1959. Under existing U.S. treaties, fish meal could be imported duty free, and Peruvian exporters took full advantage. While the American fisheries tried to secure tariffs on Peruvian fish meal, they failed.[205] As a result of these developments, the industry suffered from a precipitous drop in the price due to a decreased demand and an increased supply.

"Within the short space of time of less than six months," according to National Fisheries Institute, "this large domestic industry . . . is on the brink of economic disaster." The decrease in demand by farmers for menhaden fish meal and solubles, combined with the increase in supply from the Gulf Coast and Peru, basically destroyed the market for fish products. The price of fish meal hit a high in July 1959 of $140 per ton. This fell to $100 per ton in December and to $80-$90 per ton six months later. During the same period, the price of fish solubles fell from 28 cents per gallon in October to 14 cents per gallon in December and to 10 cents per gallon in June 1960. Likewise, the price of fish oil also dropped but less dramatically since it is not an ingredient in animal feed. In 1956, fish oil was 56 cents per gallon. The price for each gallon steadily fell each year to 53 cents in 1957, 50 cents in 1958, 43 cents in 1959, 38 cents in 1960, 31 cents in 1961, and 25 cents in 1962. At these prices for menhaden products, the fish factories began to operate at a loss during the 1960 season.[206]

During the first months of 1960, the menhaden companies in Lewes and throughout the United States still had not sold all the products from their 1959 catch. This was first time that the Fish Products Company carried over a major portion of a season's production. The Lewes factories could not control their losses and, in response, tried to cut costs. Wages to both management and fishermen were reduced, and maintenance of the vessels was held to only needed repairs. To be sure, the Lewes fish companies adopted "selective fishing" in 1960 as a response to the steady, but slower, drop in fish oil prices. To net the menhaden with the most oil, experienced fishermen concentrated on schools north of the Delaware Bay, where older, larger fish with more oil were concentrated. The industry, therefore, was clearly in trouble three seasons before the landings plunged in 1963.

While the Smith family closed the Lewes factories, it maintained limited operations in New Jersey and North Carolina, in addition to their Gulf of Mexico facilities. Reduced fishing operations along the entire Atlantic coast decreased the supply which, in turn, raised the price of the menhaden products. By the fall of 1965, the market price of fish meal had rebounded to $135 per ton. Despite this, the Smith family did not restart their Lewes operation or expand their limited operations elsewhere. The five Smith siblings met in October 1970 to decide whether to consolidate their Atlantic operations or to sell all the factories. Among several suggestions for a possible location for the merger of the Atlantic operations, Otis suggested Lewes but wanted to wait until he arranged for a study about cleaning up the air pollution and odors. One of the Smith sisters advised waiting until they received a final bid from an interested buyer. Until they had an offer in hand, the Smith family deferred the decision on consolidation of their East Coast operations. That final offer never came.[207]

The Atlantic menhaden fishery began to improve in the early 1970s but never came close to the record abundance of the glory years of the 1950s. Despite the slight improvement, the Smith siblings sold J. Howard Smith, Inc. to a British corporation, Hansen Trust Limited, in December 1973 for $32 million. With its purchase, the British conglomerate acquired more than one hundred boats and a dozen plants, organizing the assets into Seacoast Products Incorporated. Hanson retained several managers of J. Howard Smith, Inc., offering Otis Smith a five-year contract to manage the Gulf of Mexico operations. Hanson's plans for its eighty-three acres of Lewes beachfront with two plants that had been idle for over seven years were unknown. A Wilmington newspaper hoped, "Perhaps a new approach at Lewes might restore some of the menhaden catch to that port."[208]

While Hansen continued the menhaden business elsewhere, it did not immediately restart its Lewes operation. The Hansen Trust's acreage on the Lewes beachfront was prime commercial property as the only industrially zoned area on the Delaware coast between the Maryland border and the Chesapeake and Delaware Canal. Rumors about possible uses of the site, all related to future offshore oil productions, were flying. However, the only "activity" was a six-alarm fire that destroyed the "old Otis Smith pier" on a Saturday night in July 1974. Fires had always been a threat to menhaden facilities because fish oil and other flammable materials had impregnated their wooden structures through years of use. This fire was notable for its damage. It burned out of control for nearly ninety minutes, virtually destroying the 540-foot pier and causing over $1 million in damages.[209]

The fire also destroyed any immediate plans Hansen Trust may have had for the Lewes property and, in December 1974, sold the property to Joseph I. Goldstein, owner of Star Enterprises and chairman of the board of a real estate firm managing the property. Rumors about using the Lewes bayfront as a base for drilling operations continued. At the time, Goldstein vehemently denied any intention to use the land for an oil business. After conceding that he had "talked" with oil companies, he "said that there are no agreements, contracts or leases with the oil companies *at present*" [emphasis added]. Rather, he outlined possible innocuous uses, such as a boat ramp, small boat storage facility, or a maritime museum. The buildings became the Delaware Maritime Research Center with nineteen tenants, some using the old bunk houses as offices and the old factories and storage buildings as warehouses. A year later, Star Enterprises applied for state and federal permits to launch "one of the most extensive underwater land projects ever applied for in the state." In its proposal, the company explained that it would dredge 1.6 million cubic yards of material to restore the depth to 20 feet, construct 1,373 feet of bulkheads, and restore four piers, including the one destroyed the previous summer. The state held up approval because it needed more complete information on the proposed use of the new piers. Moreover, Lewes residents and officials were concerned about an oil-related industry moving onto its beaches. As opposition began to develop, Star Enterprises withdrew its application.[210]

A decade had passed since the fish factories closed, and neither the current owner nor the Delaware Maritime Research Center tenants renting the buildings had expressed any interest in fish reduction factories. It was now clear to all that the once dominant menhaden fishing industry would never return. The loss to the Lewes economy was substantial. In 1959, the Fish Products Company and the Seacoast Products Company had 175 onshore employees, including 125 factory workers, with a payroll of more than $1 million dollars. Otis Smith had thirty-six boats, about 630 fishermen, and a combined payroll exceeding $2.2 million. In 1967, after the plants closed and fishing stopped, the payroll for the few remaining onshore employees dropped to $100,000. Lewes population in 1960 was 3,025; it fell 15.3 percent to 2,563 in 1970. In addition, Lewes lost the economic benefit from businesses that provided goods and services to the fish factories, such as those "grubbing the fish boats." This was just one of several economic blows that struck Lewes beginning in the 1950s. In 1954, the Diamond State Poultry Company was found guilty of shipping adulterated chickens and shuttered its large chicken processing plant that employed hundreds. A major military base, which had a relationship with Lewes similar to what the Dover Air Force Base had with Dover, was being decommissioned. Nationally, the country endured the brief but severe Eisenhower Recession of 1958, the worst national economic downturn between 1945 and 1970. The town would be able to withstand these economic blows only if its largest industry, Otis Smith's fish plants, remained healthy. But with the menhaden industry dead, Lewes needed a new industry to revive the dwindling economy.[211]

Chapter 17

Historic Charm of Lewes Emerges

Tourism soon filled the economic void left when the last menhaden factory closed. The foundation for a tourist economy began to be laid a half century earlier, following World War I. The construction of a highway from Wilmington, ninety miles to the north, and the widespread use of the automobile in the 1920s, made it easier to reach Lewes. The first organized voice to promote Lewes to vacationers was the town's chamber of commerce, in December 1925. Lewes briefly had a board of trade from 1912 to 1916, but no other group arose to replace it until the chamber was formed a decade later. To promote the town as a vacation destination, Lewes gave the fledging organization $500. This organization sparked an interest in tourism that slowly grew throughout the interwar period until it became a political force in the late 1930s. But tourism and the fish factories were always at cross purposes.[212]

The chamber quickly focused on the menhaden plants' pollution and its damage to tourism by forming in 1926 a Pollution Committee to appear before the town council and "protest against the fisheries companies dumping their refuse [from processing menhaden oil] or gerry [sic] into the bay thereby polluting the waters of our bathing beach." According to the chamber, this reflected "several complaints" to the town commission objecting to the slurry polluting the harbor. The citizens warned that "unless immediate steps are taken by the Fisheries Companies to stop this, it is likely that some drastic action will be taken." When a local newspaper reported that "bathers . . . are complaining about the water being so dirty and filthy" and "unfit for bathing," Lewes could lose its appeal as a potential tourist destination. The following week, probably at the chamber's insistence, the newspaper immediately retracted the comments about the present condition of the beach and offered that the chamber's position referred to the pollution of earlier years. Indeed, the newspaper wrote, "Lewes Beach is one of the finest beaches along the Atlantic Coast." Despite the chamber's downplaying of the current condition of the beaches, its pollution committee sought assistance of the federal government whose inspector "notified the fisheries companies to take care of the fish refuse." No real change resulted from this initial effort to curtail the polluted waters flowing from the menhaden plants. Summer cottage owners and residents continued to press the town board to stop the fish factories from dumping the residue from the manufacture of fish oil and fish scrap into the bay. A fish house manager admitted to polluting the water but pledged that it would stop as soon as they built a basin to store the slurry.[213]

The chamber of commerce folded in 1930. Six years later a second one arose, also with an expressed interest in enhancing Lewes' tourist economy, and the commissioners again appropriated money for promotion of the town. Besides supporting the chamber, the town also awarded Joseph McSweeney $135 for a pamphlet extolling Lewes' "historical mater [sic] . . . to help the merchants of the town put it across." The *Delaware Coast Press* editorialized, "Lewes has in the past few years begun to awaken to its possibilities as an outstanding point of interest as the 'oldest town in the first state . . . .'" It endorsed the proposal of "capitalizing on the historic charm of Lewes – 'ye olden city by the sea' . . . [while lamenting] the latent possibilities in this regard." The town commissioners joined the chorus when it sent a resolution to the state highway department endorsing a road to Cape Henlopen: "We believe this road . . . by making easily accessible the point of Cape Henlopen, with its historic lighthouse ruins, excellent surf fishing, and unique constant moving sand dunes, would draw a great number of tourists to Lewes and Rehoboth." In Pennsylvania, newspaper advertisements for vacation lodgings in this "Summer Paradise" promoted its boating, fishing, deep sea fishing, and many historical interests.[214]

The growth of sport fishing, too, was attracting vacationers. Following World War I, sport fishing was nearly non-existent in Lewes, with only a half dozen boats taking parties on Atlantic excursions. The industry soon grew, attracting thousands of deep-sea fishermen from New York, New Jersey, Pennsylvania, and Delaware. A milestone for tourism was the start of the Lewes Anglers Association in 1936. Sport fishermen, however, viewed the menhaden plants with particular disdain. They believed that the seines were trapping game fish and that the wastewater was likewise destroying the fish. The fishermen would often use the menhaden companies as a convenient excuse for any small catches.

Meanwhile, another recognition of Lewes as a potential tourist location came from the state in 1931, when it built the Zwaanendael Museum to celebrate the 300th anniversary of the first European settlement in Delaware by the Dutch. In May 1941, the *Delaware Pilot* ran a four-page supplement promoting tourist activities and services in Lewes. These efforts to attract visitors, however, were blunted by the menhaden factories. The unpleasant outputs from the factories into both the air and the water made Lewes a "hard sell," especially for return visitors.[215]

World War II crushed the vigorous attempt to build an economy based on tourism. The war's first impact on Lewes tourism was the building of Fort Miles, a major military base on Cape Henlopen located beyond the fish factories. The purpose of this fortification was to guard the mouth of Delaware Bay from the German surface fleet and to repel any amphibious assault on the state's unguarded Atlantic coast. The multi-million-dollar national defense fortress, the largest defense project on the Atlantic Coast, would cover over 1,000 acres and house large surface-to-surface guns in bunkers buried in the Cape's dunes. The artillery was supported by a series of aiming towers strewn along the ocean coast. In support of this defensive network, the U.S. government installed anti-aircraft batteries to defend the bunkers and added the necessary auxiliary services needed to support a major military fortress. At its peak, Fort Miles housed more than 2,200 soldiers. Theoretically, this military fortification could sink any surface ship approaching Delaware Bay or nearby Atlantic shores.[216]

The initial plans and authorization for this "National Defense project" dated to 1934. Work on the fortification, however, did not begin until June 1940, when army surveyors staked off an area along the beach. In the first half of 1941, the U.S. Army built not only an 1800-foot pier into the bay but also a way across the road over the giant sand dunes to connect this pier with the road leading to Lewes. As construction began on Fort Miles in April 1941, the military closed to civilian use the paved road that had opened just four years earlier to make Cape Henlopen more accessible for tourists. Three months later, in August 1941, the military barred all residents and visitors from Cape Henlopen, and patrols started to enforce the restriction. A *Delaware Coast News* columnist commented that construction "seems to spell 'finis'" to tourism on Cape Henlopen.[217]

If tourists had no place to go, they also had no place to stay. Construction workers assigned to Fort Miles, beginning in 1941, soon overwhelmed all readily available housing. Responding to the demand, the Lewes Board of Commissioners announced,

> In order to provide homes, rooms and board for the men who will come to Lewes on the contemplated defense construction at the Cape Henlopen reservation, the commissioners of Lewes request that all persons having houses, apartments, rooms, and rooms and board, to register same at the mayor's office.

With all available housing in Lewes occupied, workers sought accommodations in Rehoboth Beach, commuting daily the eleven miles to Fort Miles. As the laborers vacated their housing with the completion of construction of the fort before the end of the year, accommodations became more available but never to the pre-construction levels.[218]

Besides no place to go and no place to stay, the tourists also had no way to get there. As part of the overall war effort, the government imposed strict rationing of gasoline and tires. Tires were the first item to be rationed. The government ordered a temporary ban on the sale of tires just four days after Pearl Harbor and began to severely ration tires a month later. Gasoline rationing started in Delaware and sixteen other eastern states in May 1942 and spread nationally in December. Almost everyone received "A" stamps, which were worth three to five gallons of gasoline per week for vital personal activities such as shopping, attending church, and going to the doctor. To save both tires and fuel, a national speed limit of 35 miles per hour was imposed. Three weeks after Pearl Harbor, Washington banned the sale of any automobile to civilians. A month later, automobile factories switched to producing tanks, aircraft, weapons, and other military products. By the beginning of the 1942 tourist season, visitors had no means to get to Lewes.[219]

After World War II, efforts to promote tourism sputtered along. In the summer of 1951, the chamber of commerce published 25,000 copies of a pamphlet that fully described many sites of historical interest, as well as a description of modern, everyday Lewes. It extolled an excellent beach and the unsurpassed recreational opportunities for fishing and boating. Visitors to the Zwaanendael Museum increased from 7,900 in 1952 to over 11,000 in 1957. As the menhaden industry reached its height in 1959, the Delaware State Development Department touted, "The colorful port and resort of Lewes, where the waters of the Delaware Bay join those of the mighty Atlantic, is preparing for what promises to be its biggest summer season." The chamber recommended in April 1947 that all promotional materials include the saying "The First Town in the First State" and in 1956 acknowledged the 325th anniversary of the settlement of Lewes with a four-day celebration in conjunction with Independence Day. The *Delaware Coast Press* printed in 1959 and every year thereafter *The Vacationer*, a multipage supplement that listed the various tourist-oriented businesses in the Rehoboth and Lewes areas.[220]

In April 1961, Marjorie F. Virden, a columnist for the *Delaware Coast Press*, wrote a front-page column about Lewes. After briefly discussing the economic benefits of tourism, she wondered:

> What Lewes, a truly historical town, this year celebrating the 330th year of its founding, can get of this 'windfall' depends on our community itself, by which we mean its recognition of the values of tourist business, its attitude toward tourists, and the steps it takes to stimulate and promote this business . . . . We here in Lewes have the makings of a terrific touristy center.

Even Otis Smith, president of Fish Products, saw the benefits of a future in tourism. In 1960, Smith predicted that Lewes would become a much larger resort and that Rehoboth Beach would grow north until it would reach Lewes. He envisioned that the entire coastal section of southeastern Sussex County would be one vast resort.[221]

No matter how many seeds of tourism were strewn, they could not take root and thrive in a menhaden garden. The most formidable obstacle to Otis Smith's vision of a vast resort was his fish factories – or at least the odors and other pollutants they emitted. Since 1883, those by-products had been a concern of residents and proprietors alike, the residents complaining and the proprietors promising the most modern and pollutant-free factories. In the 1950s, Fish Products and Seacoast Products Company adopted several pollution controls, such as advanced dryers, screens to capture air pollutants, and recycled factory waters for reuse. When the latest technology never fulfilled the promises, the factory owners acknowledged that some odor would always ooze from the plants and dismissed the complaints by calling it "the smell of money."[222]

Three factors spurred the growth of tourism in Lewes. First, in 1952, the opening of the first span of the Chesapeake Bay Bridge—connecting the Baltimore and Washington, D.C. metropolitan areas to the Eastern Shore—made accessible the Atlantic beaches of Delaware and Maryland to an explosion of vacationers. Second, the Cape May-Lewes Ferry began operation twelve years later, transporting tourists from New Jersey and New York. The third and greatest impetus for tourism was the opening of Cape Henlopen State Park, also in 1964. This reversed the impact of the establishment of Fort Miles in 1941, when the military banned all civilians from Cape Henlopen. The tourists now had 5,200 acres of recreational reasons that beckoned them. The continuing pledges from Otis Smith to reopen the factories undoubtedly kept some Lewestowners from fully committing themselves to a tourist economy. However, change did come with each passing year. With it, a charming, picturesque, historic town replaced a blue-collar, industrial, smelly city.

Paradoxically, the menhaden factories of the twentieth century, with their foul air and unpleasant by-products, turned Lewes into the quaint, attractive city we now behold in the twenty-first. Hazel Brittingham, a Lewes native and local historian, has frequently claimed that the fish factories made Lewes into what it is today. As she would explain, Lewes' relationship with menhaden was far different from Detroit's with the automobile or Pittsburgh's with steel. The relationship was based on the daily smell of 2 million dead fish. At the height of the menhaden industry in the 1950s, tourism was booming elsewhere on the Delaware and Maryland coasts south of Lewes and on the New Jersey shore to the north. Wherever the builders, second-home owners, hoteliers, and tourist service providers went, they razed the old buildings to make way for new ones.[223]

This was reflective of the times when "urban renewal projects" replaced the "old" with the "new." According to one professor of architecture, "If something was old and obsolete, the logical move was to get rid of it." But in Lewes, the odors and other pollutants kept developers away, which meant they did not raze the eighteenth- and nineteenth-century buildings, Victorian mansions, and twentieth-century bungalows and replace them with condos, restaurants, and hotels, to serve tourists.[224]

With the departure of the fish factories in the 1960s, the tourist industry began to blossom. By sheer coincidence, this growth occurred simultaneously with a shift in the national awareness of the importance of historic preservation. This is reflected in the popularity of First Lady Jacqueline Kennedy's well-publicized renovation of the White House and the enactment in 1966 of the National Historic Preservation Act. This statute provided the first public funding for the National Trust for Historic Preservation and established the Advisory Council on Historic Preservation, State Historic Preservation Offices, and the National Register of Historic Places. The builders and those who adopted Lewes as their own brought with them a desire to restore and revive rather than to destroy and replace, thus making Lewes a delightful tourist destination today.

Appendix A

Factories by year, 1883-1894

FACTORY	1883	1884	1885	1886	1887	1888	1889	1890	1891	1892	1893	1894
Luce Brothers	■	■	■	■	■	■	■	■	■	■	■	
Samuel S Brown & Co.	■	■	■	■	■	■	■	■	■	■	■	
Delaware Fish Oil & Fertilizer Company												
American Fisheries Co.												
United States Menhaden Oil & Guano Co.												
The Fisheries Co.												
Menhaden Fishing Co.												
Lewes Fisheries Co.												
Delaware Fish Oil Co.												
Coast Fish Oil & Fertilizer Co.												
Lewes Oil & Chemical Co.												
Breakwater Fisheries Co.												
Breakwater Fisheries Co. (leased to Hayes & Anderton)												
Coast Fish Oil & Fertilizer Co. (leased to Hayes & Anderton)												
Lewes Fertilizer Co.												
Consolidated Fisheries Co.												
Atlantic Fisheries Co.												
Fish Products Co.												
Seacoast Products Co.												

Appendix A

Factories by year, 1895-1906

FACTORY	1895	1896	1897	1898	1899	1900	1901	1902	1903	1904	1905	1906
Luce Brothers	■	■										
Samuel S Brown & Co.	■	■										
Delaware Fish Oil & Fertilizer Company		■	■	■								
American Fisheries Co.				■	■	■						
United States Menhaden Oil & Guano Co.				■	■	■	■					
The Fisheries Co.						■	■	■	■	■	■	■
Menhaden Fishing Co.												
Lewes Fisheries Co.												
Delaware Fish Oil Co.												
Coast Fish Oil & Fertilizer Co.												
Lewes Oil & Chemical Co.												
Breakwater Fisheries Co.												
Breakwater Fisheries Co. (leased to Hayes & Anderton)												
Coast Fish Oil & Fertilizer Co. (leased to Hayes & Anderton)												
Lewes Fertilizer Co.												
Consolidated Fisheries Co.												
Atlantic Fisheries Co.												
Fish Products Co.												
Seacoast Products Co.												

Appendix A

Factories by year, 1907-1918

FACTORY	1907	1908	1909	1910	1911	1912	1913	1914	1915	1916	1917	1918
Luce Brothers												
Samuel S Brown & Co.												
Delaware Fish Oil & Fertilizer Company												
American Fisheries Co.												
United States Menhaden Oil & Guano Co.												
The Fisheries Co.	■											
Menhaden Fishing Co.		■	■	■								
Lewes Fisheries Co.						■	■	■	■		■	
Delaware Fish Oil Co.						■	■	■	■	■	■	
Coast Fish Oil & Fertilizer Co.						■	■	■	■	■	■	■
Lewes Oil & Chemical Co.												■
Breakwater Fisheries Co.												
Breakwater Fisheries Co. (leased to Hayes & Anderton)												■
Coast Fish Oil & Fertilizer Co. (leased to Hayes & Anderton)												
Lewes Fertilizer Co.												
Consolidated Fisheries Co.												
Atlantic Fisheries Co.												
Fish Products Co.												
Seacoast Products Co.												

Appendix A

Factories by year, 1919-1930

FACTORY	1919	1920	1921	1922	1923	1924	1925	1926	1927	1928	1929	1930
Luce Brothers												
Samuel S Brown & Co.												
Delaware Fish Oil & Fertilizer Company												
American Fisheries Co.												
United States Menhaden Oil & Guano Co.												
The Fisheries Co.												
Menhaden Fishing Co.												
Lewes Fisheries Co.												
Delaware Fish Oil Co.												
Coast Fish Oil & Fertilizer Co.												
Lewes Oil & Chemical Co.	■	■										
Breakwater Fisheries Co.												
Breakwater Fisheries Co. (leased to Hayes & Anderton)		■	■	■	■							
Coast Fish Oil & Fertilizer Co. (leased to Hayes & Anderton)		■	■	■	■							
Lewes Fertilizer Co.						■	■	■	■	■		
Consolidated Fisheries Co.											■	■
Atlantic Fisheries Co.												
Fish Products Co.												
Seacoast Products Co.												

Appendix A

Factories by year, 1931-1942

FACTORY	1931	1932	1933	1934	1935	1936	1937	1938	1939	1940	1941	1942
Luce Brothers												
Samuel S Brown & Co.												
Delaware Fish Oil & Fertilizer Company												
American Fisheries Co.												
United States Menhaden Oil & Guano Co.												
The Fisheries Co.												
Menhaden Fishing Co.												
Lewes Fisheries Co.												
Delaware Fish Oil Co.												
Coast Fish Oil & Fertilizer Co.												
Lewes Oil & Chemical Co.												
Breakwater Fisheries Co.												
Breakwater Fisheries Co. (leased to Hayes & Anderton)												
Coast Fish Oil & Fertilizer Co. (leased to Hayes & Anderton)												
Lewes Fertilizer Co.												
Consolidated Fisheries Co.	■	■	■	■	■	■	■	■	■	■	■	■
Atlantic Fisheries Co.												
Fish Products Co.									■	■	■	■
Seacoast Products Co.												

Appendix A

Factories by year, 1943-1954

FACTORY	1943	1944	1945	1946	1947	1948	1949	1950	1951	1952	1953	1954
Luce Brothers												
Samuel S Brown & Co.												
Delaware Fish Oil & Fertilizer Company												
American Fisheries Co.												
United States Menhaden Oil & Guano Co.												
The Fisheries Co.												
Menhaden Fishing Co.												
Lewes Fisheries Co.												
Delaware Fish Oil Co.												
Coast Fish Oil & Fertilizer Co.												
Lewes Oil & Chemical Co.												
Breakwater Fisheries Co.												
Breakwater Fisheries Co. (leased to Hayes & Anderton)												
Coast Fish Oil & Fertilizer Co. (leased to Hayes & Anderton)												
Lewes Fertilizer Co.												
Consolidated Fisheries Co.	■	■	■	■	■	■	■	■	■	■	■	■
Atlantic Fisheries Co.												
Fish Products Co.	■	■	■	■	■	■	■	■	■	■	■	■
Seacoast Products Co.												

Appendix A

Factories by year, 1955-1967

FACTORY	1955	1956	1957	1958	1959	1960	1961	1962	1963	1964	1965	1966
Luce Brothers												
Samuel S Brown & Co.												
Delaware Fish Oil & Fertilizer Company												
American Fisheries Co.												
United States Menhaden Oil & Guano Co.												
The Fisheries Co.												
Menhaden Fishing Co.												
Lewes Fisheries Co.												
Delaware Fish Oil Co.												
Coast Fish Oil & Fertilizer Co.												
Lewes Oil & Chemical Co.												
Breakwater Fisheries Co.												
Breakwater Fisheries Co. (leased to Hayes & Anderton)												
Coast Fish Oil & Fertilizer Co. (leased to Hayes & Anderton)												
Lewes Fertilizer Co.												
Consolidated Fisheries Co.												
Atlantic Fisheries Co.												
Fish Products Co.	■	■	■	■	■	■	■	■	■	■	■	
Seacoast Products Co.												■

Endnotes

Introduction

1. Carol E. Hoffecker, *Delaware: The First State* (Wilmington, DE: The Middle Atlantic Press, 1989), [17].

2. Rachel Carson as quoted in Donald McCann, "The Smell of Menhaden in the Morning," *Delmarva Quarterly* (Autumn 2008), 59; John Frey, *The Men All Singing: The Story of Menhaden Fishing* (Virginia Beach VA: Donning Company, 1978), 18; H. Bruce Franklin, *The Most Important Fish in the Sea* (Washington DC: Shearwater Books, 2007), 206-208; Atlantic States Marine Fisheries Commission, *Amendment 3 to the Interstate Fishery Management Plan for Atlantic Menhaden* (November 2017), 10.

3. Atlantic States Marine Fisheries Commission, *Amendment 3*, 10, 18.

4. Jane Harrison, "Menhaden: Big Questions About Little Fish," *Seacoast*, North Carolina Sea Grant, 4 (Winter 2020), n.p. ncseagrant.ncsu.edu; Atlantic States Marine Fisheries Commission, *Amendment 3*, ii; Frey, *The Men All Singing,* 18; Franklin, *The Most Important Fish in the Sea*, 206-208.

5. "A Brief History of America's Menhaden Fishery," Saving Seafood website, 3. savingseafood.org.

6. Typescript of *Delaware Pilot* article, November 17, 1894, Box 1, Folder 19, Gilbert P. Smith's History File, Papers of Gilbert Smith (2009.32), Lewes Historical Society, Lewes, DE.

7. David Celelski, "Menhaden Stories: In the Spirit of Capt. Eugene Gore," Brunswick County's Black History Symposium – 2020, Southport NC, February 7-9, 2020. African American _ Menhaden Stories: In the Spirit of Capt. Eugene Gore presented (2020) - YouTube; Rob Leon Greer, The Menhaden Industry of the Atlantic Coast, Appendix III to the Report of U.S. Commissioner of Fisheries for 1914 (Washington, DC: Government Printing Office, 1917), 29.

Chapter 1. The Fish No One Knows

8. Leonard C. Roy, "Menhaden—Uncle Sam's Top Commercial Fish," *National Geographic* 117, no. 4 (June 1949), 813; Frye, *The Men All Singing*, 15-16; Wikipedia, "Atlantic Menhaden," Atlantic menhaden - Wikipedia.

9. Atlantic States Marine Fisheries Commission, *Amendment 3*, 6, 16; Fred C. June, "The Menhaden Fishery of the United States," U.S. Department of the Interior, Fish and Wildlife Service, Fishery Leaflet No. 521, (August 1961) in Fred June Reports, 1958-1962, Scientific Studies

on The Fishing, Processing and Uses of Menhaden, 1952-1970, Papers of Otis Smith (2009-32), Lewes Historical Society, Lewes, Delaware; U. S Geological Survey, *Atlantic Continental Shelf and Slope of the United States*, Geological Survey Professional Paper 529-4 (Washington, DC: Government Printing Office, 1966), A-9.

10. Franklin, *The Most Important Fish in the Sea*, 45-47; June, "The Menhaden Fishery of the United States"; Atlantic States Marine Fisheries Commission, *Amendment 3*, 4,

11. Franklin, *The Most Important Fish in the Sea*, 48; Kent S. Price, Jr., "The Great Menhaden Fishery of Lewes, Delaware," ed. John C. Kraft and Robert L. Salisbury, *Transactions of the Delaware Academy of Science*, 1 and 2 (1970 and 1971),187-190; Frye, *The Men All Singing*, 7-8; Harrison, "Menhaden: Big Questions About Little Fish"; Atlantic States Marine Fisheries Commission, *Amendment 3*, 4, 12, 20-21.

12. Jane Hofve, "Menhaden: The Most Important Fish You Never Heard Of," *Dogs Naturally Magazine* (March 15, 2020), n.p. dogsnaturallymagazine.com; G. Brown Goode, *A History of the Menhaden* (New York: Orange Judd, 1880), 10; Atlantic States Marine Fisheries Commission, *Amendment 3*, 6.

13. Franklin, *The Most Important Fish in the Sea*, 8.

Chapter 2. Catching and Processing Menhaden

14. "To Catch a Menhaden," *Oilways, A Magazine for Industry* 26, (December 1960), 15-18; Frye, *The Men All Singing*, 32-36.

15. "To Catch a Menhaden," *Oilways*, 15-18; [John R. Lowry], "Get Ready Below!," ed. Anne R. Davis (typescript) 31, 33, Lewes Historical Society, Lewes, DE.

16. Frye, The Men All Singing,183; Barbara J. Garrity-Blake, The Fish Factory: Work and Meaning for Black and White Fishermen of the American Menhaden Industry (Knoxville: University of Tennessee Press, 1994), 19, 102-104.

17. Frey, *The Men All Singing*, 184.

18. Garrity-Blake, *The Fish Factory*, 88.

19. Frey, *The Men All Singing*, 184.

20. *Delaware Coast Press*, August 14, 1958; Reports of the Department of Commerce, 1914, H. Doc. 1505, 406-408; *The Morning News* (Wilmington, DE), May 20, 1983; "To Catch a Menhaden," *Oilways*, 15-18.

21. Rob Leon Greer, *The Menhaden Industry of the Atlantic Coast*, 17, 21-22; Garrity-Blake, *The Fish Factory*, p. 24.

22. Robert Hunter Orr, *A Small-town Boyhood in the First State* (Denver CO: Sassafras Press, 1999), 32.

23. *Carteret County News-Times*, October 11, 1955, as quoted in Steve

Goodwin, *Beyond the Crow's Nest: The Story of the Menhaden Fishery of Carteret County, NC* (Atlantic Beach NC: Eastern Offset Printing Co., 2017), 131.

Chapter 3. Black and White Work Side-by-Side

24. Garrity-Blake, *The Fish Factory*, 16, 43-45; David Cecelski, "Music All Over the Ocean," August 8, 2017, Core Sound Lectures, davidcecelski.com.

25. Steve Goodwin, *Beyond the Crow's Nest*, 57; *Delaware Coast News*, May 26, 1928, October 27, 1939, December 9, 1954; *Delaware Pilot*, July 8, 1938, October 27, 1939.

26. Bobby Chambers, Interview, December 15, 2009, Raising the Story: Menhaden Fishing Collection: An Oral History of the Outer Banks and Down East, N.C., Recording : OH 2013.001.267 (carolinacoastalvoices.com); Goodwin, *Beyond the Crow's Nest*, 91.

27. Goodwin, Beyond the Crow's Nest, 91.

28. [Lowry], "Get Ready Below!," 9; Frye, *The Men All Singing*, 115; Goodwin, *Beyond the Crow's Nest*, 91, 141; *Richmond Times Dispatch*, June 8, 1952, June 29, 1952.

29. "A Brief History of America's Menhaden Fishery," Saving Seafood, 3; *News Journal* (Wilmington, DE), February 26, 1997; *The Daily Times* (Salisbury, MD), March 31, 1999; Bobby Chambers, Interview, December 15, 2009; *The Morning News* (Wilmington, DE), May 20, 1983.

30. Garrity-Blake, *The Fish Factory*, 14-15, 47-49; *Delaware Coast News*, March 27, 1931; Frey, *The Men All Singing*, 52; Market News Leaflet 52: Menhaden Fish Oil Prices – New York City, 1950-1962 and January 1963, Bureau of Commercial Fisheries, February 1963, "Market Analysis for Fish Meal and Fish Oil, 1959-1962," Materials Relating to the Management and Operations of the Smith Companies, 1954-1970, Otis Smith Papers; *News Journal* (Wilmington, DE), September 3,1993.

31. *Milford Chronicle*, April 26, 1929; "Where There's Menhaden, There's Quinn," *Fish Meal & Oil Industry*, April 1950, 8 as quoted in Goodwin, *Beyond the Crow's Nest*, 115.

32. Garrity-Blake, *The Fish Factory*, 32-33; Latisha "Tish" Tickle, November 13, 2009, Raising the Story: Menhaden Fishing Collection: An Oral History of the Outer Banks and Down East, N.C. Recording : OH 2013.001.277 (carolinacoastalvoices.com).

33. Newspaper clipping, June 16, 1900, Judith Atkins Roberts Scrapbooks, Lewes Historical Society; Minutes, October 7, 1912, Lewes Town Commission, Lewes City Hall, Lewes, Delaware.

34. *Delaware Coast Press*, August 3, 1929, October 12, 1929, November 23, 1929; Minutes, April 27, 1927, July 6, 1937, Lewes Town Commission.

35. *Delaware Pilot*, April 6, 1939.

36. Louis A. Rickards, "Grubbing Them Fishboats," *Journal of the Lewes Historical Society*, 7 (November 2004), 9-17; *Milford Chronicle*, April 26, 1929, August 18, 1933, May 7, 1926, November 22, 1934; *Delaware Coast News*, February 28, 1936; Minutes, September 1, 1924, Lewes Town Commission; *Delaware Coast News*, July 15, 1938, December 9, 1954; Lizzie Carter, Diary, December 12, 1934, Lewes Historical Society, "Population of Lewes, DE," Population.US. For a discussion of Lizzie Carter, see Betty Grunder, "Diarist Lizzie Carter," Journal of the Lewes Historical Society, 10 (November 2007), 52-54.

37. Otis H. Smith to Josef Rosengarten, November 13, 1948, "Recruitment of German POWSs, 1945," Materials Relating to The Management and Operations of The Smith Companies in The Aftermath of World War II, 1946-1954, Otis Smith Papers; Proposed Capital Improvements for 1949, List of Capital Expenditures [1948], Supplemental Brief in Re: Section102, January 23, 1947, "Financial Correspondence, 1951-1953," Materials Relating to The Management and Operations of The Smith Companies in The Aftermath of World War II, 1946-1954, Otis Smith Papers; *Delaware Coast Press*, October 11, 1995.

Chapter 4. The Menhaden Industry in Lewes Begins

38. Ralph H. Gabriel, "Geographic Influences in the Development of the Menhaden Fishery on the Eastern Coast of the United States," *The Geographical Review*, 10 (July-December 1920), 92-97.

39. Minutes, December 12, 1882, January 4, 1883; January 5, 1883; February 9, 1883; February 23, 1883; February 7, 1898; December 29, 1897; January 26, 1897; March 1, 1897; March 8, 1897, Lewes Town Commission; Newspaper clipping, May 15, 1897, Judith Atkins Roberts scrapbooks.

40. Minutes, January 4, 1883, Lewes Town Commission; United States v. Luce et al., *The Federal Reporter*, 141 (St. Paul: West Publishing Co., 1906), 392-393. babel.hathitrust.org.

41. United States v. Luce et al., *The Federal Reporter*, 391, 394-395,396, 397, 399, 400, 401,403.

42. *New York Times*, January 9, 1898, May 26, 1900; *Lowell Sun* (Massachusetts), December 22, 1897; *Newport Daily News* (Rhode Island), March 8, 1900; Report of the Industrial Commission on Trusts and Industrial Combinations H. Rep. No. 57-182, (1902), cxxv, 683; Report of the Fisheries Company Against the Ratification of the Hay-Bond Treaty for the Improvement of Commercial Relations with Newfoundland, H. Doc 57-24, (1903), 2; Gabriel, "Geographic Influences," 98-99; *Boston Globe*, March 19, 1902.

43. *New York Times*, March 8, 1900, May 26, 1900; Newspaper clipping

dated May 19, 1900, Judith Atkins Roberts scrapbooks; *Philadelphia Inquirer,* October 25, 1907, August 18, 1901.

44. *New York Times,* March 11, 1906; *Philadelphia Inquirer,* October 25, 1907.

45. *Philadelphia Inquirer,* May 28, 1908, October 25, 1907, February 5, 1911; *Baltimore American,* September 9, 1910; *Charlotte Observer,* November 23, 1911.

46. *Catching A Million Fish...* (Lewes, DE: Coast Fish Oil and Fertilizer Co., 1913), n.p.; Minutes, January 14, 1911, Lewes Town Commission; Deed Book 178-575, Recorder of Deeds, Sussex County, Georgetown, Delaware; *Delaware Pilot,* February 13, 1911; *Philadelphia Inquirer,* July 20, 1911.

47. Minutes, December 18, 1911, Lewes Town Commission; Incorporation Record, Volume B-2, 312, Sussex County Recorder of Deeds, Georgetown, DE.; *Delaware Pilot,* January 9, 1914, December 17, 1915. The Delaware Fish Oil Company is mistakenly called the "Delaware Fisheries Company" in some official documents. See Lewes, Camp Henlopen map, RG 9200 S20 001, Small Manuscripts Collection, Short Coastal Land Co., Surveys, Plats and Maps, 1733-1954, Delaware Public Archives.

48. Dennis Forney, "Mayor James Thompson," *Journal of the Lewes Historical Society,* 2 (November 1999), 52-53; Hazel D. Brittingham, "Two Mayors Served Lewes for One-Year Terms," *Journal of the Lewes Historical Society,* 4 (November 1999), 41; William Lloyd Bevan, *History of Delaware: Past and Present* 4 (Wilmington, DE: Lewis Historical Publishing Company, 1929), 313.

49. Incorporation Record, Volume B-2, 470-477; Betty Grunder, "Outten's Lyceum," *Journal of the Lewes Historical Society,* 2 (November 1999), 48-49; *Catching a Million Fish....,*n.p.

50. Deposition of William C. Lofland, November 17, 1917, 2-5, November 17, 1917, Charles V. Jones v. Lewes Fisheries Company, Sussex County Chancery Court Case File, c. 1895-1930, Misc. Cases B-D, Delaware Public Archives, Dover, DE; *Johnson's Steam Vessels of the Atlantic Coast* (New York: Eads Johnson Publishing Company, 1917), 38, 51, 96; United States Department of the Navy, Naval Historical Center, Naval Historical Center home page, Online Library, *Dictionary of American Naval Fighting Ships (DANFS),* history.navy.mil, n.p.

51. Map of Lewes, Cape Henlopen, 1915, Shore Coastal Lands Company, Surveys, Plots and Maps, 1733-1954, Record Group 9200.520.001, Delaware Public Archives.

52. Deed Book 181; *Philadelphia Inquirer,* October 31, 1911; Judith Atkins Roberts, "Miss Lil," *Journal of the Lewes Historical Society,* 3 (November 2000), 18-19.

53. Deed Book 196, 22, exhibit A; Deed Book 132, 202-204; Deed Book 135, 56-58, *Philadelphia Inquirer*, October 31, 1911.

54. Thomas R. Ingram to Sen. Henry A. DuPont, January 18, 1912, Letters relating to Examinations and Surveys for Neptune Fishing Pier, Hearing Transcript, February 8, 1912, Correspondence Relating to Structural Permits ("B&P"), 1907-1942, Records of the Office of the Chief of Engineers (Record Group 77), Mid-Atlantic Region, National Archives and Records Administration, Philadelphia.

55. Hearing Transcript, February 8, 1912, Records of the Office of the Chief of Engineers. *Philadelphia Inquirer*, February 9, 1912

56. "2nd indorsement [sic]," Capt. L. H. Rand to Delaware Fish Oil Company, February 17, 1912, Letters relating to Examinations and Surveys for Neptune Fishing Pier, Records of the Office of the Chief of Engineers; Deed Book 200, 559-562; Deed Book 186, 396-398; Deed Book 189, 305-308.

Chapter 5. A Tale of Two Home Companies

57. *Philadelphia Inquirer*, May 6, 1917; Victor Hugo Erpf to Allen Smith, April 9, 1917, Case Number 8000-9995, Old German Files, 1909-21, Investigative Case File of the Bureau of Investigation, Record Group 65, National Archives and Records Administration, College Park, MD.

58. *Milford Chronicle*, May 2, 1919, March 14, 1919, March 21, 1919, May 2, 1919, May 23, 1919, July 18, 1919, August 1, 1919.

59. *Milford Chronicle*, July 18, 1919; September 19, 1919, November 21, 1919.

60. *Dictionary of American Naval Fighting Ships (DANFS)*, Naval Historical Center homepage for *Albert Brown* (SP-1050), *Delaware* (SP-467), *Fearless* (SP-724), *Sussex* (SP-685); Deed Book 207, 465; *Philadelphia Inquirer*, August 14, 1917; *Milford Chronicle*, August 24, 1917.

61. Summary of Testimony, 18, Commissioners of Lewes v. Breakwater Fisheries, Sussex County Chancery Court Case Files, c. 1895-1930, Misc. Cases B-D, Delaware Public Archives, 18; *Milford Chronicle*, August 31, 1917; *Newport Daily News* (Rhode Island), February 18, 1910.

62. Deed Book 209, 76-78; Minutes, September 3, 1917, Lewes Town Commission.

63. *Milford Chronicle*, June 27, 1919.

64. *Milford Chronicle*, November 2, 1917, November 30, 1917, March 14, 1918, September 15, 1918, April 11, 1919, May 16, 1919, June 13, 1919, June 20, 1919, September 5, 1919, October 1, 1920.

Chapter 6. The Lewes Fisheries Company

65. Bevan, *History of Delaware*, 4, 430-431.

66. Deposition of William C. Lofland, November 17, 1917, Charles V.

Where Menhaden Was King

Jones v. Lewes Fisheries Company, Sussex County Chancery Court Case Files, Delaware Public Archives.

67. Deposition of William C. Lofland, November 17, 1917, Charles V. Jones v. Lewes Fisheries Company, Delaware Public Archives; Cahall v. Lofland, May 6, 1921, *The Atlantic Reporter*, Vol. 114 (St. Paul: West Publishing Co., 1921), 114:14. babel.hathitrust.org.

68. Deposition of Harland M. Joseph, November 16, 1917; Deposition of Robert Pennington, November 13, 1917, Exhibit A, Charles V. Jones v. Lewes Fisheries Company, Sussex County Chancery Court Case Files, Delaware Public Archives.

69. Deposition of William C. Lofland, November 17, 1917, Charles V. Jones v. Lewes Fisheries Company, Sussex County Chancery Court Case Files, Delware Public Archives.

70. Cahall v. Lofland, *The Atlantic Reporter*, 114: 236.

71. Deposition of Robert Pennington, November 13, 1917, Cahall v. Lofland, May 6, 1921, Sussex County Chancery Court Case Files, Delaware Public Archives.

72. Deposition of William J. Thompson, November 17, 1917, Charles V. Jones v. Lewes Fisheries Company, Sussex County Chancery Court Case Files, Delaware Public Archives; Cahall v. Lofland, *The Atlantic Reporter*, 114: 238-239.

73. Cahall v. Lofland, *The Atlantic Reporter*, 114: 238-239.

74. Deposition of William C. Lofland, November 17, 1917, Deposition of Harland M. Joseph, November 16, 1917, Charles V. Jones v. Lewes Fisheries Company, Sussex County Chancery Court Case Files, Delaware Public Archives; Cahall v. Lofland, *The Atlantic Reporter*, 114: 237.

75. Charles V, Jones, Bill to Appoint Receiver Upon Dissolution, October 9, 1917, Testimony, January 2, 1923, Joint and Several Answers of Lewes Fisheries Company et. al, December 9, 1918, Suit Docket I, p.3, Charles V. Jones v. Lewes Fisheries Company, Sussex County Chancery Court Case Files, Delaware Public Archives; Bevan, *History of Delaware*, 4, 431.

76. *Milford Chronicle*, November 29, 1918, June 13, 1919, July 18, 1919, July 25, 1919, August 22, 1919, November 14, 1919, June 18, 1920, July 16, 1920.

Chapter 7. More Legal Problems for Lofland

77. Testimony, January 2, 1923, 7-8, Joint and Several Answers of Lewes Fisheries Company et. al, December 9, 1918, n.p., Suit Docket I, p.3, Charles V. Jones v. Lewes Fisheries Company, Sussex County Chancery Court Case Files, Delaware Public Archives.

78. Cahall v. Lofland, *The Atlantic Reporter*, 114: 228-229.

79. Testimony, January 2, 1923, 12-13, Charles V. Jones v. Lewes Fisheries Company, Sussex County Chancey Court Case Files, Delaware Public Archives.

80. Joseph L. Cahall, "Receiver's Report and Petition for Compensation," n.d., 7; Charles V. Jones v. Lewes Fisheries Company, Sussex County Chancery Court Case Files, Delaware Public Archives.

81. Charles V. Jones vs. Lewes Fisheries Company, Suit Docket I, 3-4; Joseph L. Cahall, "Receiver's Report and Petition for Compensation," 2, 4, 7, Charles V. Jones v. Lewes Fisheries Company, Sussex County Chancery Court Case Files, Delaware Public Archives.

82. Cahall v. Lofland, *The Atlantic Reporter*, 115: 460. babel.hathitrust.org; Henry Ridgely, Testimony, January 2, 1923, 18, Joseph L. Cahall, "Receiver's Report and Petition for Compensation," n.d., 8, Charles V. Jones v. Lewes Fisheries Company, Sussex County Chancery Court Case Files, Delaware Public Archives; Carter, Diary, August 19, 1917 – December 22, 1924, Lewes Historical Society.

82. Cahall v. Lofland, *The Atlantic Reporter*, 115: 460. babel.hathitrust.org; Henry Ridgely, Testimony, January 2, 1923, 18, Joseph L. Cahall, "Receiver's Report and Petition for Compensation," n.d., 8, Charles V. Jones v. Lewes Fisheries Company, Sussex County Chancery Court Case Files, Delaware Public Archives; Carter, Diary, August 19, 1917 – December 22, 1924, Lewes Historical Society.

83. Henry Ridgely, Testimony, January 2, 1923, 18; Charles V. Jones v. Lewes Fisheries Company, Sussex County Chancery Court Case Files, Delaware Public Archives; Carter, Diary, May 7, 1921, Lewes Historical Society.

84. Cahall v. Lofland, *The Atlantic Reporter*, 114: 229-234, 239-240.

85. Joseph L. Cahall, "Receiver's Report and Petition for Compensation," n.d., 21, Charles V. Jones v. Lewes Fisheries Company, Sussex County Chancery Court Case Files, Delaware Public Archives; Cahall v. Lofland, *The Atlantic Reporter*, 114: 229-234, 239-240; *Milford Chronicle*, September 2, 1921.

86. *Milford Chronicle*, September 2, 1921 December 14, 1923; June 22, 1922; Deed Book 230, 547-548; Henry Ridgely, Testimony, January 2, 1923, 38-39, Charles V. Jones v. Lewes Fisheries Company, Delaware Public Archives.

87. *Milford Chronicle*, March 24, 1922, April 7, 1922, April 14, 1922, April 28, 1922, May 5, 1922; Death Certificate, Roll 20, Frame 979, Department of Heal and Social Service, Vital Statistics, RG 1500.21, Delaware Public Archives. Ancestry.com has indexed this certificate under "William Charles Laffant."

88. *News Journal* (Wilmington, DE) May 6, 1922; File Number 124105,

Annual Report 1924, Menhaden Products Corporation, Division of Corporation, Secretary of State, Dover, Delaware; Robert C. Mathers, Delaware Department of State, to Author, September 9, 2009; Minutes, May 2, 1922, Lewes Town Commission; Incorporation Record E-5, 24-241, Recorder of Deeds, Sussex County; *Milford Chronicle*, February 23, 1923.

89. Joseph L. Cahall, "Receiver's Report and Petition for Compensation," n.d., 15; Henry Ridgely, Testimony (January 2, 1923), 2, 38-39; Correspondence to Hiram Rodney Burton, December 1922, Charles V. Jones v. Lewes Fisheries Company, Sussex County Chancery Court Case Files Delaware Public Archives.

90. Joseph L. Cahall, Final Report, December 9, 1924, Charles V. Jones v. Lewes Fisheries Company, Sussex County Chancery Court Case Files, Delaware Public Archives.

Chapter 8. It's in the Lease

91. Minutes, August 4, 1919, October 6, 1919, November 3, 1919, Lewes Town Commission; *Milford Chronicle*, October 31, 1919; Testimony of Witnesses (May 1, 1923), 104, 227, 151, Commissioners of Lewes v. Breakwater Fisheries Company, Sussex County Chancery Court Case Files, Delaware Public Archives.

92. Minutes, October 13, 1919, November 3, 1919, Lewes Town Commission; *Philadelphia Inquirer*, October 27, 1919; Testimony of Witnesses, (May 1, 1923), 226, Commissioners of Lewes v. Breakwater Fisheries, Sussex County Chancery Court Case Files, Delaware Public Archives.

93. Roberts, "Miss Lil," 18-19; Testimony of Witnesses (May 1, 1923), 113-114, Commissioners of Lewes v. Breakwater Fisheries Company, Sussex County Chancery Court Case Files, Delaware Public Archives; Deed Book 227, 563-565; Deed Book 220, 122-124.

94. Testimony of Witnesses (May 1, 1923) 111-112, Commissioners of Lewes v. Breakwater Fisheries Company, Sussex County Chancery Court Case Files, Delaware Public Archives.

95. Deed Book 209, 76-78.

96. Testimony of Witnesses (May 1, 1923), 204, 276, 274, Commissioners of Lewes v. Breakwater Fisheries Company, Sussex County Chancery Court Case Files, Delaware Public Archives.

97. Testimony of Witnesses, (May 1, 1923) 187-189; Bill in Equity to Reform a Deed (February 12, 1920) Suit Docket I, 129-133, Commissioners of Lewes vs. Commissioners of Lewes v. Breakwater Fisheries Company, Sussex County Chancery Court Case Files, Delaware Public Archives.

98. Bill in Equity to Reform a Deed, Suit Docket I, 129-133, Commissioners of Lewes vs. Breakwater Fisheries Company Sussex County

Chancery Court Case Files, Delaware Public Archives; *Milford Chronicle,* July 6, 1923.

99. *Milford Chronicle,* January 16, 1920, February 27, 1920, March 5, 1920.

Chapter 9: There Will Be Plenty of Fish

100. Deed Book 240, 64-66; Deed Book 305, 341-346, Incorporation Record, E-5, 272-278; Frey, *The Men All Singing,* 113-114; New York State Census, 1925, Assembly District 21, Volume 8, p. 8, line 43 from Ancestry.com.

101. Incorporation Record, F-6, 390-397, Incorporation Record G-7, 238-240.

102. Frye, *The Men All Singing,* 102, 114; "History", Box 2, Gilbert P. Smith's History File, Papers of Gilbert Smith.

103. Betty Grunder, "Mayor Otis Smith," *Journal of the Lewes Historical Society* 6 (November 2003), 7-9.

104. *Washington Post,* July 15, 1919; *Milford Chronicle,* September 15, 1922, January 19, 1923, October 26, 1923; Incorporation Record, E-5, 86-90; *Delaware Coast News,* November 23, 1929, November 2, 1929; E. L. Sherrill, III "List of Boats Owned by Smiths with Registered Lengths and Divisions Owned By," Weems, VA (August 11, 2002). Lewes Historical Society.

105. Frye, *The Men All Singing,* p, 114; *Delaware Coast Press,* December 9, 1954; James Tunnell to Seacoast Products, December 3, 1954, "Consolidated Fisheries Acquisition, November – December 1954," Materials Relating to the Management and Operations of the Smith Companies, 1954-1970, Otis Smith Papers.

106. *Milford Chronicle,* October 22, 1920, August 12, 1920, September 9, 1920, August 18, 1922, May 11, 1923.

107. *Milford Chronicle,* August 8, 1924, August 15, 1924, October 24, 1924; August 21, 1925, July 24, 1925, October 16, 1925, October 30, 1925, October 26, 1928.

108. *Delaware Coast News,* March 27, 1931; *Milford Chronicle,* June 30, 1933; Minutes, June 6, 1932, August 1, 1931, Lewes Town Commission.

109. *Delaware Coast News,* May 20, 1938.

110. Press Releases, January 14, 1947, February 16, 1949, February 3, 1954, Information Services, Department of Interior, Fish and Wildlife Services; fws.gov; "Sardine Fishery of California," *Nature* (May 16, 1953), 872.

111. Press Releases, February 3, 1954, April 11, 1956, April 29, 1958, March 3, 1961, Fish and Wildlife Service; *Delaware Coast News,* September 30, 1954, May 29, 1958; *Plain Dealer* (Cleveland, Ohio), March 25,

1954.

112. Press Releases, February 3, 1954, April 11, 1956, March 3, 1961, Fish and Wildlife Service; *Delaware Coast Press*, May 29, 1958.

Chapter 10. Something Fishy in Politics

113. Forney, "Mayor James Thompson," 52; Barbara W, Vaughan, "Lewes Mayor Ulysses W. Hocker: 1931-1935," *Journal of the Lewes Historical Society* 10 (November 2007), 49-50; Minutes, June 6, 1932, August 1, 1933, Lewes Town Commission; *Delaware Coast News*, December 2, 1932.

114. Gary Grunder, "Mayor William E. Walsh," *Journal of the Lewes Historical Society* 7 (November 2004), 31-32; Bevan, *History of Delaware*, 4, 334; *Delaware Coast News*, January 10, 1935.

115. Hazel Brittingham, "Mayor David Walter Burbage," *Journal of the Lewes Historical Society* 3 (November 2000), 59; *Milton Chronicle*, June 15, 1935.

116. Minutes, December 23, 1935, Lewes Town Commission; Deed Book 300, 271-273.

117. *Delaware Coast News*, January 10, 1935.

118. *Delaware Coast News*, November 25, 1938; *Delaware Pilot*, November 24, 1938; Minutes, January 27, 1936, Lewes Town Commission; Deed Book 300, 352-354; Deed Book 300, 341-346.

119. *Delaware Coast News*, January 10, 1935; March 27, 1936.

120. Minutes, November 17, 1938, Lewes Town Commission; Transcript of Public Hearing, February 8, 1939, Case #1859, Correspondence Relating to Structural Permits ("B&P"), 1907-1942, Records of the Corps of Engineers; *Delaware Pilot*, November 25, 1938.

121. Midge Yearly, "Paul F. Carpenter: Lewes Visionary," 22 *Lewes History: The Journal of the Lewes Historical Society*, 7; *Morning News* (Wilmington, DE), September 29, 1923; *Evening Journal* (Wilmington, DE), November 18, 1930; *News Journal* (Wilmington, DE), March 10, 1928, February 17, 1971.

122. *Delaware Coast News*, November 25, 1938; *Delaware Pilot*, November 24, 1938; Minutes, January 3, 1938, Lewes Town Commission.

123. Franklin Brittingham Papers (2005.12), Lewes Historical Society; *Delaware Coast News*, December 2, 1938.

124. *Journal-Every Evening* (Wilmington, DE), November 29, 1938, as reprinted by *Delaware Coast News*, December 2, 1938; *Delaware Coast News*, December 2, 1938.

125. *Delaware Coast News*, December 9, 1938; November 25, 1938.

126. *Delaware Pilot*, December 8, 1938; *Delaware Coast News*, December 9, 1938; *Morning News* (Wilmington, DE), December 6, 1938.

Chapter 11. The People Speak

127. *Delaware Coast News*, December 9, 1938, *Morning News* (Wilmington, DE), December 6, 1938.

128. *Delaware Coast News*, December 9, 1938.

129. *Delaware Coast News*, December 16, 1938.

130. *Delaware Coast News*, December 16, 1938, December 23, 1938, December 30, 1938.

131. Minutes, December 24, 1938, Lewes Town Commission; *Delaware Coast News*, December 30, 1938; Brittingham Papers, Lewes Historical Society.

132. Brittingham Papers, Lewes Historical Society.

133. *Delaware Coast News*, December 20, 1938.

134. *Delaware Coast News*, January 5, 1939; Brittingham Papers, Lewes History Society; *Delaware Pilot*, December 27, 1938, January 12, 1939; Minutes, June 3, 1939, Lewes Town Commission.

135. *Evening Journal* (Wilmington, DE), January 9, 1939; *Morning News* (Wilmington, DE), January 9, 1939; *Delaware Coast News*, February 10, 1939, March 24, 1939.

Chapter 12. The Fight Continues

136. Record Card, Engineer Department, Case #1859, Records of the Corps of Engineers.

137. John W. Marshal to Major C. W. Burlin, December 31, 1938; Hugh F. Gallagher et al. to Major C. W. Burlin, December 29, 1938; Record Card, Case #1859, Records of the Corps of Engineers.

138. Irvin S. Maull to Major C. W. Burlin, December 30, 1938; Paul F. Carpenter to Major C.W. Burlin, January 5, 1939, Case #1859, Records of the Corps of Engineers.

139. Gilbert P. Smith to War Department, December 31, 1938, Record Card, Engineer Department, U.S. Army, Case #1859, Records of the Corps of Engineers.

140. Transcript of Public Hearing, February 8, 1939, Case #1859, Records of the Corps of Engineers.

141. Transcript of Public Hearing, February 8, 1939, Case #1859, Records of the Corps of Engineers.

142. Transcript of Public Hearing, February 8, 1939, Case #1859, Records of the Corps of Engineers; *Delaware Coast News*, February 10, 1939.

143. C. W. Burlin to Menhaden Company, April 4, 1939, Menhaden Company to C. W. Burlin, April 9, 1939, Case #1859, Records of the Corps of Engineers; *Delaware Coast News*, February 10, 1939; *Delaware News Press*, April 21, 1939.

144. Howard M. Long to United States Engineers, September 29, 1942, T. H. Jett, Menhaden Company to U.S. Army Engineers, November 23, 1942, B.C. Dunn to Menhaden Company, December 16, 1942, Case #1859, Records of the Corps of Engineers.

145. Howard M. Long to United States Engineers, September 29, 1942, Case #1859, Records of the Corps of Engineers; *Delaware Coast News*, November 25, 1938; December 9, 1938.

146. *Delaware Coast News*, December 9, 1938.

147. "Cemetery at Lewes, Delaware," n.d. n.p.; "Lewes Sailors Cemetery, 1939-1941," Attorney General Files, Delaware Public Archives, Dover, DE; *Delaware Coast News*, April 7, 1939; April 21, 1939.

148. Delaware Code, Title 7, Chap. 51. delcode.delaware.gov; *Delaware Pilot*, June 15, 1939; Thomas H. Hayes to Thomas R. Ingram, May 3, 1939, "Lewes Sailors Cemetery, 1939-1941, Attorney General Files, Delaware Public Archives; *Delaware Coast News*, April 7, 1939, May 5, 1939, December 9, 1938.

149. *Delaware Pilot*, June 15, 1939; *Delaware Coast News*, May 5, 1939, May 19, 1939.

150. *Delaware Pilot*, June 15, 1939.

151. Leon deValenger, "Report on the Historical Background of the 'Unknown Sailors Cemetery' Lewes Delaware," February 17, 1940, Swaanendael Papers, William J. Cohen Collection, Lewes Historical Society Archives; Houston Wilson to James M. [sic] Morford," June 29, 1939, Houston Wilson to James R. Morford, July 8, 1939, James R. Morford to Houston Wilson, October 6, 1939, "Lewes Sailors Cemetery, 1939-1941," Attorney General Files, Delaware Public Archives.

152. Houston Wilson to James R. Morford, October 6, 1939, "Lewes Sailors Cemetery, 1939-1941," Attorney General Files. Delaware Public Archives; DeValinger, Jr., "Report on the Historical Background of the 'Unknown Sailors Cemetery' Lewes, Delaware," February 17, 1940, William J. Cohen Collection, Lewes Historical Society.

153. DeValenger, "Report on the Historical Background of the 'Unknown Sailors Cemetery' Lewes Delaware," William J. Cohen Collection, Lewes Historical Society; Houston Wilson to James R. Morford, April 19, 1941, James R. Morford to Mary Wilson Thompson, June 11, 1941, "Lewes Sailors Cemetery, 1939-1941," Attorney General Files, Delaware Public Archives; "Minutes of the Delaware Society for Antiquities, June 16, 1941," Records of the Delaware Society of Antiquities, Delaware Historical Society, Wilmington, DE.

Chapter 13. A Critical Industry Survives

154. Frye, *The Men All Singing*, 196-197; J. Howard Smith to William Stuart Snow, July 18, 1942, William Stuart Snow to Senator Warren W.

Barbour, March 10, 1943, "American Fishing Association Cooperative, 1941-1945," Promotion of the Menhaden Industry, 1941-1945 & 1959-1973, Otis Smith Papers.

155. C. B. Platt to [?] Bland, December 12, 1941; AFAC Bulletin 84, February 17, 1942, "American Fishing Association Cooperative, 1941-1945," Otis Smith Papers.

156. John Frye, *The Men All Singing*, 106-116.

157. Erskine B. Wood to Schuyler Otis Bland, February 1, 1943; W. Ancrum to Otis Smith, June 3, 1942; William Stuart Snow to Sen. Warren W. Barbour, March 10, 1943; William Stuart Snow to J. Howard Smith, November 27, 1942, "American Fishing Association Cooperative, 1941-1945," Otis Smith Papers.

158. Press Release, June 19, 1943, Department of Interior, Coordinator of Fisheries.

159. *The Daily Whale*, November 25, 1989; Executive Order 9381, Amendment of Executive Order No. 9250, Entitled ``Providing for the Stabilization of the National Economy'," September 25, 1943,, Executive Orders and Proclamations, Franklin D. Roosevelt Library, Hyde Park, New York.

160. AFAC [American Fishing Association Cooperative] Bulletin #78, no date, "American Fishing Association Cooperative, 1941-1945," Otis Smith Papers.

161. The Minutes of Special Meeting of the Board of Directors of Fish Products Company, November 9, 1942, "World War II," Management & Operations of The Smith Companies, 1946-1975, Otis Smith Papers.

162. Michael Morgan, *World War II and the Delaware Coast* (Charleston, SC: History Press, 2016), 114; Delaware *Coast News*, June 16, 1944; *Sussex Countian*, March 25, 1945; November 8, 1945; July roster, "Recruitment of German POWS, 1945," Otis Smith Papers.

163. William Snow to J. Howard Smith, March 10, 1942, "American Fishing Association Cooperative, 1941-1945," Otis Smith Papers.

164. Advance Release, September 3, 1943, Office of War Information. fws.gov.

165. Press Releases, August 6, 1943, June 19, 1943, Information Services, Department of Interior; Advance Release, September 3, 1943, Office of War Information, fws.gov.

166. *Delaware Coast News*, May 21, 1943, June 11, 1943, October 29, 1943.

Chapter 14: Organizing the Smith Companies

167. Frye, *The Men All Singing*, p. 102; Otis Smith to Colonel T. H. Setliffe, April 12, 1961, "Management and Operation Issues, 1954-

1962," Materials Relating to The Management and Operations of The Smith Companies, 1954-1970, Otis Smith Papers; *Daily Times* (Salisbury, MD), January 5. 1950.

168. Minutes, "Smith Family Meeting Regarding Corporate Interests, 1946, 1950, 1953, 1958, 1966-1973," Materials Relating to Meetings of the Smith Family Regarding Their Corporations, 1946-1973, Otis Smith Papers; Frye, *The Men All Singing*, p. 102.

169. *The News and Observer* (Raleigh, NC), June 12, 1960; *The 1928 Calyx*, Washington and Lee Yearbook, Washington and Lee University Digital Archives. The Calyx, 1928 (yearbook) (wlu.edu).

170. Thomas M. Kerrigan, Chronological Record of Labor Relations Developments RE: J. Howard Smith, Inc. and Affiliated Companies, September 16, 1963, "Materials Relating to Contract Negotiations, 1947-1973, Predominant 1950-1969," Labor Management Relations, 1942-1973, Otis Smith Papers.

171. Thomas M. Kerrigan, Chronological Record of Labor Relations Developments RE: J. Howard Smith, Inc. and Affiliated Companies, September 16, 1963; Walter Mercer to Gilbert P. Smith, July 26, 1950; J. Howard Smith, Inc. vs. International Fur and Leather Workers of the United States and Canada, Final Judgment, February 15, 1954, "Materials Relating to Contract Negotiations, 1947-1973, Predominant 1950-1969," Otis Smith Papers; *Richmond Times Dispatch*, July 19, 1952.

172. Robert G. Kelley to Otis H. Smith, September 7, 1956, "Materials Relating to Contract Negotiations, 1947-1973, Predominant 1950-1969," Labor Management Relations, 1942-1973, Otis Smith Papers.

173. [Otis Smith's meeting notes for August 3, 10, and 21, 1956], "Materials Relating to Contract Negotiations, 1947-1973, Predominant 1950-1969," Labor Management Relations, 1942-1973, Otis Smith Papers.

174. [Otis Smith meeting Notes, October 5, 1956], "Materials Relating to Contract Negotiations, 1947-1973, Predominant 1950-1969," Labor Management Relations, 1942-1973, Otis Smith Papers.

175. Tom Kerrigan to C.M. Cubbage, May 28, 1957, "Materials Relating to Contract Negotiations, 1947-1973, Predominant 1950-1969," Labor Management Relations, 1942-1973, Otis Smith Papers.

176. Tom Kerrigan to C.M. Cubbage, May 28, 1957, "Materials Relating to Contract Negotiations, 1947-1973, Predominant 1950-1969," Labor Management Relations, 1942-1973, Otis Smith Papers.

177. Thomas M. Kerrigan, Chronological Record of Labor Relations Developments RE: J. Howard Smith., Inc. and Affiliated Companies, September 16, 1963; "Suggested Remarks to be Delivered by Mr. Otis Smith on the Occasion of the Opening of the 1958 Menhaden Season," n.d., "Materials Relating to Contract Negotiations, 1947-1973, Predominant 1950-1969," Labor Management Relations, 1942-1973,

Otis Smith Papers.

178. Unknown author, Memorandum, September 4, 1958; Otis Smith to C. M. Cubbage, September 9, 1958; Thomas M. Kerrigan to Boat Captains, n.d., "Materials Relating to Contract Negotiations, 1947-1973, Predominant 1950-1969," Labor Management Relations, 1942-1973, Otis Smith Papers.

179. Unknown author, Memorandum, September 4, 1958; Otis Smith to C. M. Cubbage, September 9, 1958; DRAFT AGREEMENT, n.d.; Copies of Union Contracts with Boat Captains; Thomas Kerrigan to Harold M. Hoffman, November 18, 1959; Thomas M. Kerrigan to Otis Smith, July 1961, Thomas M. Kerrigan to Boat Captains, n.d., "Materials Relating to Contract Negotiations, 1947-1973, Predominant 1950-1969," Labor Management Relations, 1942-1973, Otis Smith Papers.

180. Petition signed by 14 captains, n.d., "Boats, 1957-1967," Materials Relating to The Management and Operations of the Smith Companies, 1954-1970; Otis Smith to Larry Clarke, April 19, 1962; Otis Smith to David Nelson Sutton, March 26, 1962, "Materials Relating to Contract Negotiations, 1947-1973, Predominant 1950-1969," Labor Management Relations, 1942-1973, Otis Smith Papers.

181. Petition of Engineers, July 9, 1961; International Boatmen's Union of the Seafarers International Union to Sea Coast Products Co. et. al., June 20, 1963; Thomas M. Kerrigan, Chronological Record of Labor Relations Developments RE: J. Howard Smith., Inc. and Affiliated Companies, September 16, 1963; Notice, October 17, 1963; Notice, October 30, 1963, "Materials Relating to Contract Negotiations, 1947-1973, Predominant 1950-1969," Labor Management Relations, 1942-1973, Otis Smith Papers.

Chapter 15. Research and Development

182. *Public Press and Delaware Coast Press*, September 18, 1947.

183. Frye, *The Men All Singing,* p. 171-172; Greer, *The Menhaden Industry of the Atlantic Coast,* 17.

184. Franklin, *The Most Important Fish in the Sea,* 121; Frye, *The Men All Singing,* pp. 174, 175.

185. Frye, *The Men All Singing,* p. 174; Franklin, *The Most Important Fish in the Sea,* p. 121; Notes, November 11, 1957, "Boats, 1957-1967," Materials Relating to The Management and Operations of the Smith Companies, 1954-1970; Otis Smith Papers.

186. Frye, *The Men All Singing,* pp. 135-136, 176; Press Releases, August 1, 1944, Information Service, Department of the Interior.

187. Frye, *The Men All Singing,* p. 176; *Delaware Coast Press,* July 7, 1955; Earl F. Ritter, "Fish Spotting," *Journal of the Lewes Historical Society* 3 (November 2000), 35-37.

188. *Delaware Coast Press*, August 27, 1953, September 22, 1955, June 28, 1956; Barbara W. Vaugh, "College of Marine Studies," *Journal of the Lewes Historical Society* 5 (November 2002), 71.

189. J. Howard Smith Reorganization Plan, May 15, 1953; "Financial Correspondence, 1951-1953," Materials Relating to the Management and Operations of the Smith Companies in the Aftermath of World War II, 1946-1954; "Confidential Report, Summary as of December 10, 1958, of All Reports," unnumbered report, Reports from Robert C. Ernst, 1950-1967, Otis Smith Papers; *News Journal* (Wilmington, DE), November 12, 1959; January 23, 1960.

190. *Delaware Coast Press*, May 31, 1962; *News Journal* (Wilmington, DE), November 12, 1959, January 23, 1960.

191. *Sussex Countian* (Georgetown, DE), March 3, 1960; *Delaware Coast Press*, March 31, 1960; Frye, *The Men All Singing*, p 116; *Omaha World Herald*, January 22, 1955; *The Advocate* (Baton Rouge); *Fish Protein Concentrate: Hearings Before a Subcommittee of the Interstate and Foreign Commerce Committee*, 87th Cong, 2nd session, August 8-9, 1962; *Delaware Coast Press*, February 9, 1967.

Chapter 16: The Future Looked Promising

192. *The Newark Advocate* (Newark, OH), October 29, 1959.

193. News Release, March 1963 (ca), Fish and Wildlife Service; *Salisbury Times*, August 15, 1964, August 27, 1964; *Morning News* (Wilmington, DE), July 20, 1964, July 18, 1964, August 15, 1964, August 27, 1964.

194. *Morning News* (Wilmington, DE), March 11, 1965, July 20, 1966.

195. *Morning News* (Wilmington, DE), January 24, 1967, August 27, 1964, March 11, 1965, February 8, 1968.

196. *Time* magazine, June 16, 1967; *Morning News* (Wilmington, DE), August 27, 1964, March 11, 1965, January 24, 1967, February 8, 1968; *Salisbury Times* (Maryland), July 22, 1964; *Evening Times* (Cumberland, MD), April 4, 1968.

197. National Sea Grant and Program Act of 1966, Pub. L. 89-688, 33 USC 1112 (2020).

198. June, "The Menhaden Fishery of the United States," U.S. Department of the Interior, Fish and Wildlife Service, Fishery Leaflet No. 521, (August 1961) in Fred June Reports, 1958-1962, Papers of Otis Smith, Lewes Historical Society.

197. National Sea Grant and Program Act of 1966, Pub. L. 89-688, 33 USC 1112 (2020).

198. June, "The Menhaden Fishery of the United States," U.S. Department of the Interior, Fish and Wildlife Service, Fishery Leaflet No. 521,

(August 1961) in Fred June Reports, 1958-1962, Papers of Otis Smith, Lewes Historical Society.

199. "Overfishing," National Geographic, April 27, 2010. nationalgeographic.com.

200. Press release, n.d., "Conservation Service Award, U.S. Department of the Interior, 1962," Management and Operations of the Smith Companies, 1954-1970, Otis Smith Papers; *Morning News* (Wilmington, DE), May 26, 1962; *Delaware Coast Press*, May 31, 1962.

201. J. Steele Culbertson to Stewart L. Udall, March 3, 1961, "National Fisheries Institute, Jan-Mar, 1960-1973," Materials Concerning the National Fisheries Institute, 1960-1973, Otis Smith Papers.

202. *News Journal* (Wilmington, DE), July 26, 1966; Fred C. June and J. Lockwood Chamberlain, "Role of the Estuary in the Life History and Biology of the Atlantic Menhaden," *Proceedings of the Gulf and Caribbean Fisheries Institute, Eleventh Annual Series* (November 1958), 41-45. Copy in June Reports, 1958-1962, Otis Smith Papers.

203. Price, "The Great Menhaden Fishery of Lewes, Delaware," p. 190; Maryland Department of Environment, "The Story of the Chesapeake Bay." mde.maryland.gov; Franklin, *The Most Important Fish in the Sea*, 136-140.

204. *Sandpiper*, August 1987, Hazel Brittingham Papers, copy provided to author by Hazel Brittingham.

203. Price, "The Great Menhaden Fishery of Lewes, Delaware," p. 190; Maryland Department of Environment, "The Story of the Chesapeake Bay." mde.maryland.gov; Franklin, *The Most Important Fish in the Sea*, 136-140.

205. J. Steele Culbertson to Stewart Udall, March 3. 1961, "National Fisheries Institute, Jan-Mar, 1960-1973," Materials Concerning the National Fisheries Institute, 1960-1973. Otis Smith papers.

206. J. Steele Culbertson to Stewart Udall, March 3. 1961, "National Fisheries Institute, Jan-Mar, 1960-1973," Materials Concerning the National Fisheries Institute, 1960-1973. Otis Smith papers.

207. Otis Smith Papers; Minutes of Meeting Held October 5, 1970, at Port Monmouth, N.J., "Smith Family Meeting Regarding Corporate Interests, 1946, 1950, 1953, 1958, 1966-1973," Materials Relating to Meetings of the Smith Family Regarding Their Corporations, 1946-1973, Otis Smith Papers.

208. *News Journal* (Wilmington, DE), January 4, 1974, January 8, 1974; *Salisbury Times* (Maryland) January 6, 1974; Frye, *The Men All Singing*, 116-117.

209. *News Journal* (Wilmington, DE), July 22, 1974.

210. *News Journal* (Wilmington, DE), December 10, 1974, August 8,

1975, October 9, 1975.

211. G.L. Hettich, Jr. to Otis Smith, March 18, 1960; 1967 Accounts Payable, "Cash Accounts, Smith Corporations, 1958-1967," Materials Relating to The Management and Operations of the Smith Companies, 1954-1970, Otis Smith Papers; *Salisbury Times* (Maryland), July 16, 1964, October 13, 1964; *News Journal* (Wilmington, DE), July 9, 1960, July 20, 1966; Unites States v. Diamond State Poultry Company, 125 F. Supp 617 (D. Del. 1954).

Chapter 17. The Historic Charm of Lewes Emerges

212. Minutes, March 8, 1912, May 16, 1916, December 1, 1925, Minute Book, Lewes Chamber of Commerce, Delaware Public Archives; Minutes, December 15, 1925, Lewes Town Commission.

213. *Milford Chronicle*, July 16, 1926, July 23, 1926; Minutes, August 9, 1926, Lewes Town Commission.

214. Minute Book, March 17, 1936, Lewes Chamber of Commerce, Delaware Public Archives; Minutes, May 2, 1927, April 23, 1933, July 1, 1935, Lewes Town Commission; *Delaware Coast Press*, July 15, 1936; *Delaware County Daily Times* (Upper Darby Township, PA), May 31, 1938; *Evening Standard* (Uniontown, PA), August 21, 1936.

215. *Delaware Pilot*, May 30, 1941.

216. Morgan, *World War II and the Delaware Coast*, pp. 26-29.

217. *Delaware Coast News*, February 21, 1941, May 22, 1941, August 15, 1941; Morgan, *World War II and the Delaware Coast*, 26-29.

218. *Delaware Coast News*, March 14, 1941, January 22, 1943; Morgan, *World War II and the Delaware Coast*, 29-30.

219. University of North Carolina School of Education, "World War II on the Home Front: Rationing." learnnc.org.

220. *Delaware Pilot*, May 30, 1941; *Delaware Coast Press*, July 19, 1951, October 2, 1952, September 15, 1957, February 9, 1956, May 7, 1959; *Delaware Public Press and Delaware Coast News*, April 24, 1947; *News Journal* (Wilmington, DE), July 6, 1960.

221. *Delaware Coast Press*, April 27, 1961.

222. *Cape Gazette* (Lewes, DE), September 29, 2015; David Cecelski, "Capt. Eugene W. Gore: The Smell of Money," Listening to History News, *The News and Observer* (Raleigh, NC), June 9, 2002. Gore, Eugene W.: The Smell of Money | NCpedia.

223. In numerous conversations with the author, Hazel Brittingham offered this view of the fish factories making Lewes what it is today. She also repeated this interpretation publicly during the comment period of some Lewes Historical Society's Lecture Series programs.

224. *Washington Post*, September 11, 2015.

Selected Bibliography

Books and Articles

Atlantic States Marine Fisheries Commission. Atlantic Menhaden Plan Development Team. *Amendment 3 to the Interstate Fishery Management Plan for Atlantic Menhaden.* November 2017.

Brittingham, Hazel D. "Two Mayors Served Lewes for One-Year Terms." Journal of the Lewes Historical Society, 24 (November 2001): 41-44.

Franklin, H. Bruce. *The Most Important Fish in the Sea.* Washington, DC: Shearwater Books, 2007.

Forney, Dennis. "Mayor James Thompson." *Journal of the Lewes Historical Society,* 2 (November 1999): 52-55.

Frey, John. *The Men All Singing: The Story of Menhaden Fishing.* Virginia Beach, VA: Donning Company, 1978.

Garrity-Blake, Barbara J. *The Fish Factory: Work and Meaning for Black and White Fishermen of the American Menhaden Industry.* Knoxville: University of Tennessee Press, 1994.

Goodwin, Steve. *Beyond the Crow's Nest: The Story of the Menhaden Fishery of Carteret County, NC.* Atlantic Beach, NC: Eastern Offset Printing Co., 2017.

Grunder, Betty. "Outten's Lyceum." *Journal of the Lewes Historical Society*, 2 (November 1999): 45-49.

Harrison, Jane. "Menhaden: Big Questions About Little Fish." North Carolina Sea Grant. *Seacoast* 4 (Winter 2020), n.p. ncseagrant.ncsu.edu.

Morgan, Michael. *Hidden History of Lewes.* Charleston, SC: The History Press, 2014.

_____. *World War II and the Delaware Coast.* Charleston, SC: The History Press, 2016.

"To Catch a Menhaden." *Oilways, A Magazine for Industry.* December 1960. 15-18

Rickards, Louis A. "Grubbing Them Fishboats." *Journal of the Lewes Historical Society,* 7 (November 2004): 9-17.

Ritter, Earl F. "Fish Spotting" *Journal of the Lewes Historical Society,* 3 (November 2000): 35-37.

Roberts, Judith Atkins. "Miss Lil." *Journal of the Lewes Historical Society,* 3 (November 2000): 18-19.

Vaughan, Barbara W. "Camile." *Journal of the Lewes Historical Society* 4 (November 2001): 16-20.

_____. "College of Marine Studies." *Journal of the Lewes Historical Society* 4 (November 2002): 71-73.

_____. "Lewes Mayor Ulysses W. Hocker: 1931-1935." *Journal of the*

Lewes Historical Society 10 (November 2007): 49-51.

Manuscript Resources

Attorney General Delaware. "Cemetery at Lewes, Delaware." Attorney General Administration Files, 1939-1941. [RG 1560.000.023] Delaware Public Archives. Dover, DE.

Carter, Lizzie. Diary. Lewes Historical Society. Lewes, DE.

Corps of Engineers, U. S Army. Correspondence Relating to Structural Permits ("B&P"), 1907-1942. Records of the Office of the Chief of Engineers (Record Group 77), Mid-Atlantic Region, National Archives and Records Administration. Philadelphia, PA.

Brittingham, Papers of Franklin. [2005.12] Lewes Historical Society. Lewes, DE.

Deed Books. Sussex County Recorder of Deeds. Georgetown, DE.

Fish and Wildlife Service, Press Releases, 1914-2019. fws.gov.

Incorporation Records. Sussex County Recorder of Deeds. Georgetown, DE.

Minutes 1883-1996. Lewes Town Commission. Lewes City Hall, Lewes, DE.

Roberts, Judith Atkins. Scrapbooks. Lewes Historical Society. Lewes, DE.

Smith, Papers of Otis. [2009.32] Lewes Historical Society. Lewes, DE.

Court Cases

Cahall v. Lofland. *The Atlantic Reporter*. St. Paul: West Publishing Co., 1921. babel.hathitrust.org.

Charles V. Jones v. Lewes Fisheries Company. Sussex County Chancery Court Case File, c. 1895-1930, Misc. Cases B-D. Delaware Public Archives. Dover, DE.

Commissioners of Lewes v. Breakwater Fisheries. Sussex County Chancery Court Case Files, c. 1895-1930, Misc. Cases B-D. Delaware Public Archives. Dover, DE.

United States v. Luce et. al. St. Paul: West Publishing Co., 1906). babel.hathitrust.org.

Index

Page numbers followed by a "*t*" indicate tables. Page numbers in bold indicate photographs.

A

Abbott, William G., 27
Advisory Council on Historic Preservation, 140
African Americans, **88**; desegregation of fishery industry and, 15–17; number in Lewes' fishery industry, 19; politicians' appeal to, 71; role in menhaden operations, 3–4; sea chantey traditions of, 9–11; as seasonal workers, 14–15; as ships' officers, 16; wives of, 18
air spotting, 121–22, 127–28
Albert Brown, 27, 31
Allison, Frank E., 74
Amalgamated Meat Cutters and Butcher Workmen of North America's Union, 115–16, 117–18, 119
American Fisheries Company, 23–24, 141*t*–147*t*
American Fishing Association Cooperative, 106–7, 108
Anderson, Katherine Lane, 27–28, 29
Anderton, Raymond J., 31–32, 46, 49, 50–51, 52
Annie Daw, 107
Associated Press, 57
Atlantic Fisheries Company, 52–53, 55–56, 61, 62, 120, 141*t*–147*t*
Atlantic Menhaden *(Brevoortia tyrannus)*, **82**. *See also* menhaden
Atlantic Navigation Company: captains' role in, 114–15; response to changes in menhaden landings, 124–25; unionization and, 116, 118–19
Atlantic Phosphate Company, 29
Atlantic States Marine Commission, 126

B

Bailey, Hodie, 16
Baker, Harvey, 61
Baylis, Edgar M., 27
Baylis, John R., 25, 33n, 41n, 51, 53–54
Beckwith, 39
Beebe, Charles D., 70, 71, 72
Bethlehem Steel, 24
blue crab fishery, 2
Bookhammer, William E., 33n, 41n, 51
Bookhammer, William H., 25, 33, 47–48, 53–54
brailing nets, 11, **97**
Breakwater, 27, 34, 35
Breakwater Fisheries Company, 31–32, 33, 41n, 46–51, 52, 56, 60, 61, 141*t*–147*t*
Brittingham, Hazel, 139
Brown, Samuel S., 21–22
Brown & Lennen, 22
Bryan, Theodore, 61, 65
bunt, 9, **92, 93, 97**, 121
Burbage, David W., 25, 27, 29, 33, 41n, 44, 61–62, 67, 70
Bureau of Commercial Marine Fisheries, 123, 126
Burlin, C.W., 74, 75
Burton, Hiram Rodney, 45
Bussells, J.E., 53

C

Cahall, Joseph L., 42, 44–45
Cape Henlopen, 79, 135
Cape Henlopen State Park, 139
Cape May, 123
Cape May–Lewes Ferry, 63, 139
capitation tax, 60, 67, 71, 72
Caroline Vineyard, 30
Carpenter, Paul F., 62–63, 65, 67, 68–69, 70, 71, 72, 73–74, 75, 77
Carter, Frank S., 44, 52–53, 65, 67–68, 70, 71, 72
Carter, Lizzie, 42–43
Cecelski, David, 14
Chambers, Bobby, 15
Chambers, Richard, 16
chanteys, 9–11, 12
Chesapeake Bay Bridge, 139
Chesapeake Bay pollution, 128–29
Citizens Committee, 70–71
City of Lewes, 27, 34, 35
Civilian Conservation Corps camp, 110
Clarke, Janice M. Smith, 113
Clarke, Larry I., 113, 116

Coast Fish Oil and Fertilizer Company, 27, 32, 33, 46, 51, 52, 56, 60, 141*t*–147*t*; sale of vessels to government by, 29; worker unrest and, 31
Cod, 39
College of William & Mary, 115
conservation, 128
Consolidated Fisheries Company, 52, 54, 55–56, 60, 65, 70, 78, **90**, 107, 109, 110, 111, 120, 141*t*–147*t*
crime, 18–19
Cronin, L. Eugene, 122
Cubbage, C.M. "Pete," 113, 116
Cubbage, Mary Gladys Smith, 113
Curtis, Charles M., 41–42

D

David W. Burbage, 27, 30
Davis, Andrian, 16
Delaware, 27, 31
Delaware Academy of Sciences, 129
Delaware Bay beaches, 21
Delaware Coast News, 18, 56, 57, 59, 61, 75, 76, 77, 136
Delaware Coast Press, 135, 138
Delaware Fish Oil and Fertilizer Company, 22, 141*t*–147*t*
Delaware Fish Oil Company, 26, 27, 30, 31, 32, 33, 47, 56, 141*t*–147*t*
Delaware Maritime Research Center, 132–33
Delaware Pilot, 25–26, 71, 72, 136
Delaware Society for the Preservation of Antiquities, 78, 80
Delaware State Development Department, 137–38
Delaware State Supreme Court, 44
deValinger, Leon, 80
Diamond State Fish Products, 53–54
Diamond State Poultry Company, 17, 133
diesel engines, 108
dip net, 11
Doxie clam factory, 17
D.W. Burbage & Company, 60

E

economy, maritime, 19–20, 109
Edwards, George, 16–17
electro-trawling, 123
elevators, 12, 49, 73, 74, **86, 87**

Elwell, James W., 35, 36
Eriksen, Cornelius M., 44n
Espionage Act of 1917, 108–9
estuary degradation, 128–29
Evans, Nathaniel H., 70

F

fall fishery, 6–7
Fearless, 27, 31
Federal Board of Mediation, 118
Federal Food and Drug Administration, 2
ferry service, 63, 139
fertilizer products, 2, 30, 106
filter feeders, 7
Fish and Wildlife Service, 57, **102**, 123, 126
fish canning plant, 75
fish communication, 123
fish meal, 1, 54, 106; foreign export of, 130; for human consumption, 123; price of, 130
fish oil, 1–2, 54, 106, 130
fish processing factories: Board of Commissioners statement on, 67–68; consolidation of, 23–24; economic impact of on Lewes, 20; federal effort to close, 22–23; health issues and, 22–23; offloading of catch at, 11–12; process of establishing, 3; seasonal workers at, 15; worker salaries, 17; by year, 141*t*–147*t*; year-round workers in, 15. *See also* fishery labor; *specific companies*
Fish Products Company, 20, 74, 75, **105**, 107, 109, 110, 113, 114, 119, 125, 128, 131, 133, 138, 141*t*–147*t*
fish scrap, 12
fish solubles, 13, 130
fish spotting, 121–22, 127–28
Fisheries Company, The, 24, 141*t*–147*t*; piers and elevators, **87**
fishery labor, **88**; crime and, 18–19; desegregation of, 16; housing and meals for, 17–18; number of, 19; prisoners of war as, 109–10; racial make-up of, 15–16; salaries, 17; as seasonal workers, 15–16; shortages during World War II, 108–9; strikes and unrest, 31; wage control during World War II, 109; wives of, 18. *See also* African Americans; fish processing factories; fishing vessel crews
fishing industry and companies: business models for, 11; "foreign" companies,

170

22, 25, 28–29, 46, 51; "home" companies, 25–27; limitations on during World War II, 111; seasonal nature of, 14–15; unionization and, 115–19. *See also* specific companies
fishing seasons, 6–7
fishing techniques, 8–11
fishing vessel crews, **99**; captains' role, 114–15; desegregation of, 15–17; as migrant workers, 14–15; salaries, 17. *See also* African Americans; fishery labor
fishing vessels, **84, 85, 86**; construction by Lewes entrepreneurs, 32–33; court case concerning sale of *Henlopen*, 40–46; modernization of, 120–21; purchases of, 27; sale and requisition during WWI, 30–31, 34–35; sale and requisition during WWII, 106–8; types in menhaden fishery, 8. *See also specific vessels*
floating factories, 24–25
Food and Drug Administration, 123
forage fish, 7
"foreign" companies: defined, 22; efforts to suppress, 28–29; land leases and, 46, 51; vs "home" companies, 25
foreign conglomerates, 23–24
foreign exporters of fish products, 130
Fort Miles, 111, 136
Franklin, H. Bruce, 7
Friendship Baptist Church, 16
Frye, John, 114

G

gasoline rationing, 137
Goldstein, Joseph I., 132
Goode, G. Brown, 7
Great Depression, 56
green flies, 23
Green Run, **103**

H

Hankin, Harry, 27
Hansen Trust Limited, 131–32
Hayes, John E., 52
Hayes, Richard C., 52, 54, 56, 61, 70, 71, 107
Hayes, Thomas H., 31–32, 46, 47, 49, 50–51, 52, 54, 56, 61, 70, 71, 78, 107
Hayes Brothers factory, 52

Hazzard, Marshall, 70, 71, 72, **91**
head tax, 60, 67, 71, 72
Helen Euphane, 107
Henlopen, 27, 34, 35; court case concerning sale of, 40–46; double sale of, 36–38
Henlopen Fish Oil and Phosphate Company, 46–47
Henlopen Guano and Fish Oil Company, 46
Hocker, Ulysses, 59
Hoffecker, Carol, 1
"home" companies, 25–27. *See also* "foreign" companies
Horsey, Thomas C., 31, 32, 33n, 41n
Horsey, Thomas R., 49
Hotel Henlopen, 34
Hotel Wilmington, 34
H.R. Humphreys, 107
Hughes, James H., 77–78
Hydraulic Phosphate Company, 29

I

Ickes, Harold L., 108, 111
identification cards, 109
Ingram, Edgar W., 26n, 31, 33, 51
Ingram, Thomas R., 26, 28, 33n, 41n, 48–49
Inland Boatmen's Union, 119
International Brotherhood of Teamsters, 115
Iron Pier, 27–28
Iron Pier hospital, 77

J

J. Howard Smith, Inc., 62, 74; background in menhaden industry, 53–54; conservation efforts of, 128; as family business, 113–14; fishing fleet, 114–15; government requisition of fishing vessels of, 107–8; material acquisition during World War II, 110; modernization efforts, 120; reduction of fishing operations by, 131; repair and winter storage facility, **104**; role in research and development, 122–23; sale of, 131–32; unionization of, 115–19
James M. Gifford, 35, 36, 38–39
James W. Elwell & Company, 35, 36
Jett, Joseph C., Jr., 67

Jett, Joseph H., 62, 76, 107
Jett, Thomas H., Jr., 67
John L. Lawrence, **84,** 108
John R. Baylis, 33
Jones, Charles V., 38, 45, 70, 72
Joseph, Harland M., 25, 37, 38, 44, 52–53
June, Fred, 126–27, 128–29

K

Kennedy, Jacqueline, 140
Kerrigan, Thomas M, 116
Kreutzer, Conradin, 123

L

labor. *See* fishery labor
labor shortages, 108–9
labor strikes, 115, 119
labor unions, 115–19
Lank, James T., 25, 35, 37
Lawrence, Lillian, 27, 46, 47, 49
Layton, Caleb, 50
Layton, Daniel J., 47–48, 50, 79
Leahy, Paul, 111
lease, for third factory, 59–66; as Board of Commissioners campaign issue, 70–72; Board of Commissioners vote on, 65–66; impact on Board of Commissioners election, 70–72; impact on mayoral election, 67; opposition to, 62–63, 68–69
leases and lease negotiations, 21–22, 25, 32; Breakwater Fisheries Company and, 46–51; as factor in mayoral elections, 60–61; foreign companies and, 46
Lennen, James, 22
Lewes, Delaware: control of beaches by, 21; crime in, 18–19; fish factories' relationship with government of, 2–3; fish factory odor in, 1, 64; "foreign" companies in, 22, 25, 28–29, 46, 51; "home" companies in, 25–27; local government structure, 60; maritime economy in, 19–20; mayoral election of 1936, 59–61; menhaden collapse impact on, 132–33; as number one port in U.S., 57–58, **102**; quarantine station in, 22–23; selection as fishery site, 21; William Penn land grant and, 79–80
Lewes and Cape May Ferry, 63, 139
Lewes Anglers Association, 75, 135
Lewes bayfront, **105**

Lewes Beach Cottage Colony, 59–61
Lewes Board of Commissioners: election of, 60, **91**; mayoral election of 1936 and, 61–62; statement on fish factories, 67–68; third factory lease and, 64, 65–66, 70–72; tourism and, 137
Lewes Chamber of Commerce, 62–64, 72; opposition to Menhaden Company pier, 73–74, 75; tourism and, 134–35
Lewes Fertilizer Company, 43, 44, 52, 141*t*–147*t*
Lewes Fisheries Company, 25, 26, 27, 29, 60, 141*t*–147*t*; directors' compensation, 40–41, 43; *Henlopen* court case and, 40–46; profitability of, 37–38; in receivership, 42; sale of, 35–37, 37; sale of vessels to government by, 34–35
Lewes Oil and Chemical Company, 37, 43, 55, 141*t*–147*t*; ships purchased by, 38–39
Lewes Sand Company, 34
Little Joe, 107
Littleton, Daniel D.J., 70
lobster fishery, 2
Lofland, Fredonia, 38
Lofland, William C., 25, 29, 39, 52, **89**; death of, 44; in double sale of *Henlopen,* 36–38, 43; sale of Lewes Fisheries Company and, 35–37; sale of vessels to government and, 34–35
Long, Howard M., 76
Lowry, John B., 16
Luce, Edward C., 21
Luce, John, 21
Luce Brothers, 21, 22, 141*t*–147*t*
Luce Brothers, 108

M

Maid of the Mist, 39
Marine Operating Company, 32–33
Marshall, Edwin C., 33
Marshall, J. Orton, 63, 64, 65, 67–68, 70, 71, 72
Marshall, John W., 73
Mary B. Garner, 27, 30, 39
Maryland Department of the Environment, 129
Maryland State Supreme Court, 50
Maull, Harry C., 26n
Maull, Irvin S., 70, 73
Maull, William, 26n

mayoral election of 1936, 59–61, 67
McMullen, Richard C., 78, 79
McSweeney, Joseph, 135
menhaden, **82**; description of, 5–6; ecological role of, 7; impact of pollution on, 129; migration patterns of, 6–7; nicknames for, 5; prices, 17, 55, 124, 130; selective fishing of, 128, 131; uses of, 1–2
Menhaden Company, 62, 107; conditions of lease with, 67–70; factories by year, 141t–147t; pier construction and, 73–76, 76n
Menhaden Fishing Company, 24–25,
menhaden landings: in 1953, **102**; in 1923-1925, 55; in 1945-1960, 57t, 58t; Atlantic Navigation's response to collapse of, 124–25; causes of decline in, 125–26; as measurement of population, 127–28; peak year for, 129–30
menhaden lifecycle, 5–6, 126–27
menhaden oil, 1–2, 54
Menhaden Products Corporation, 44
Menhaden Trust, 24
menhaden year class, 127
Middle Atlantic States Fisheries Commission, 122
Milford Chronicle, 32, 55
Morford, James R., 79, 80, 81
Morris, Albert, 22
Mustard, Lewis W., 26n, 31, 32–33, 41n
Myers, Albert Cook, 80
Myers, Fred G., 27

N

National Geographic, 127
National Historic Preservation Act, 140
National Labor Relations Board, 116
National Register of Historic Places, 140
National Trust for Historic Preservation, 140
National War Labor Board, 109
Native Americans, 1
Nature magazine, 57
Neptune Fishing Company, 28–29, 39, 47
net reels, 12, **100**
nets: brailing, 11, **97**; dip, 11; nylon, 120–21; purse seine, 1, 9, 12, **83**; reels for, 12, **100**; repair of, **101**
New England fishery, 21
Newark Advocate, 124

News Journal, 128
nitroglycerin, 106
Northumberland, 107
nylon nets, 120–21

O

omega-3 fatty acids, 2
Orr, Robert, 12
Orr, William P., Jr., 23, 26, 31, 33, 41n, 49
Outten, Elmer, 27
overfishing, 127–28

P

patents, 23
Penn, William, 21, 79–80
Pennington, Robert, 39; *Henlopen* court case and, 41, 43, 45; in purchase of Lewes Fisheries Company, 35–37
Pennsylvania Railroad, 63
Peruvian fish products, 130
Peter Stuven, 39
Philadelphia Inquirer, 24, 28
Pierce, M. Haswell, 122
piers, **86, 87**; authorization for, 28; fires on, 132; Iron Pier, 27–28; Menhaden Company application for, 73–76; in off-loading process, 11–12
pilchard fisheries, 56–57, 121
plankton, 6
pollution: in Chesapeake Bay, 128–29
Poole, Harry, 115
poultry plants, 109–10
power block, 121
press liquor, 13
Price, Kent S., Jr., 129
Price Brothers, 22n
Princess Bay, **85**
prisoners of war, 109–10
Promised Land, 107
purse boats, **92, 93, 96,** 121; aluminum, **94, 95**
purse seine net, 1, 9, 12, **83**

Q

Quarantine Station, 22–23, 77

R

reduction process, 1, 2

173

Reed, Elijah, 21
Reedville, Virginia, 21
Rehoboth, 27, 34, 35
Rehoboth Beach, 1
"Report on the Historical Background of the 'Unknown Sailors' Cemetery' Lewes, Delaware" (deValinger), 80
research ships, 122–23
Ridgely, Henry, 40–46
Ripley, Arnold C., **103**
Ripley, Eileen, **103**
Robinson, Albert W., 31, 32, 33n, 41n
Roosevelt, Franklin D., 108–9
Ross, L. Finley, 26n
Russell, William A., 27
Ryden, George, 79

S

sailors' cemetery, 77–81
Salisbury, 123
Samuel Brown, 30, 31
Samuel S. Brown & Company, 21–22, 141*t*–147*t*
sardines, 57
Schneller, Warren S., 122
sea chanteys, 9–11, 12
Sea Grant Program, 126
Seacoast Products Company, 54, **105**, 113, 114, 119, 125, 128, 133, 138, 141*t*–147*t*
Seacoast Products Incorporated, 131
Seafarers International Union, 119
selective fishing, 128, 131
Seminole, 30
Seminole Fertilizer and Oil Company, 30
share system of pay, 17
ship construction, 32–33. *See also* fishing vessels
Sickle, Henry, 46
Sickler, Harvey, 28
Smith, Gilbert, 53, 74, 75, 107
Smith, Gilbert Porter II, 113
Smith, Harvey Ward, 113, 114, 115, 117
Smith, J. Howard, 53, 106, 113
Smith, Otis, **103**; air spotting and, 121–22; background of, 53; on conservation, 128; contract with Hansen Trust International, 131–32; on menhaden landings, 124–25; modernization efforts of, 120; role in family business, 113–14; on sale of Consolidated Fisheries, 54; on tourism, 138; union negotiations and, 115–16, 117
Smith Research and Development Corporation, 122–23, 126, 128
sport fishing, 135
Star Enterprises, 132–33
State Historic Preservation Offices, 140
Sterling, 108
stick water, 13
striker boat, 9
summer fishery, 6–7
Sussex, 27, 31
Suthard, Edward, 61, 70, 71, 72, **91**

T

Thompson, James T., 26–27, 26n, 29, 31, 47, 48–49, 59
Thompson, Mary Wilson, 64–65, 78–79, 80, 81
Thompson, William J., 25
Time magazine, 125
tom weight, 9
"Tomb of the Unknown Sailor," 78
tourism, 62; growth of in Lewes, 139–40; impact of fisheries pollution on, 134–35
Townsend, John G., 77
Tunnell, Ebe W., 26
Tunnell, James M., 37, 42
Tyler, Melvin, 115

U

union dues, 118
unionization, 115–19
United States Menhaden Oil and Guano Company, 24, 141*t*–147*t*
University of Delaware College of Marine Studies, 122
University of Delaware Marine Laboratory, 122
Unknown Sailors' Cemetery, 77–81
urban renewal, 139
U.S. Army, 111, 136
U.S. Army Corps of Engineers, 28–29, 73, 74
U.S. Coast Guard, 73, 74, 107, 109
U.S. Department of the Interior, 124, 128
U.S. Navy, 111; in development of air spotting, 121; negotiation in ship purchases, 34–35

V

Vacationer, The, 138
Vessels, John M., 26n, 31, 32, 33n, 41n, 51
Virden, Joseph E., 30
Virden, Thomas, 65, 75
Virden, William H., 31, 32, 33n, 41n
Virden House, 34
Virginia Fisheries Company, 30, 46–47, 48

W

wage controls, 109
Walsh, William E., 59–61, 62–63, 64, 65
Walton, Robert J., Jr., 44n
Warner, Edmund, 79
Weldon lumber mill, 10–11
wet-rendering, 13
whale oil, 2
Wharton, Joseph, 24
Wharton School of Business, 24
Wicomico River boat facility, **104**, 113
William G. Abbott and Company, 27, 33
Wilson, Houston, 79–80
Wolfe, William E., 31n
women, 18
World War I: impact on menhaden industry, 30; sale and requisition of vessels by government during, 30–31, 34–35; ship construction ventures and, 32–33; worker unrest following, 31
World War II, 56; impact on tourism, 136; labor shortages during, 108–9; material acquisition during, 110–11; menhaden processing as critical industry during, 2, 106; prisoners of war as labor during, 109–10; rationing during, 137

Z

Zwaanendael Museum, 136, 137

About the Author

Thomas Elton Brown had a thirty-year career at the National Archives and, for the last thirteen, managed Archival Services for the Center for Electronic Records. He has authored twenty academic articles and presented over fifty papers at professional conferences on archival issues related to electronic records. These writings earned him inclusion *The Encyclopedia of Archival Writers, 1515-2015*, a compendium of profiles of 150 major authors on archival topics during the past 500 years. He is a Distinguished Fellow of the Society of American Archivists, the profession's highest individual honor; recipient of the Career Achievement Award from I-ASSIST, an international professional association of data archivists and data librarians; is a Certified Archivist (C.A.); served on the Delaware Heritage Commission, 2013-2021; and is the Distinguished Alumni for 2019 of Oklahoma State University's History Department. Upon retirement from the National Archives, he volunteered as a docent, processing archivist, and researcher for the Lewes Historical Society, where he served as a trustee from 2011-2017. He has an M.A. History (1971) and Ph.D. History (1974) from Oklahoma State University.